MADE IN THE
SHADE

MADE IN THE
SHADE

A Collection of Recipes by the
Junior League of Greater
Fort Lauderdale, Inc.

Photography by Andrew Itkoff

*The Junior League of Greater Fort Lauderdale, Inc. is an organization of women committed
to promoting voluntarism and to improving the community through the effective action and leadership
of trained volunteers. Its purpose is exclusively educational and charitable.*

This cookbook is a collection of favorite recipes,
which are not necessarily original recipes.

Made In The Shade
**A Collection of Recipes by the
Junior League of Greater Fort Lauderdale, Inc.**

Library of Congress Catalog Number: 98-066544
ISBN: 0-9604158-1-5

Edited, Designed and Manufactured by
Favorite Recipes® Press
an imprint of

FRP™

P.O. Box 305142, Nashville, Tennessee 37230
800.358.0560

Managing Editor: Mary Cummings
Art Director: Steve Newman
Book Project Manager: Debbie Van Mol
Cover and Book Design: Bruce Gore
Photography: Andrew Itkoff
Food Stylist: Howard Craig Plotkin
Project Production: Sara Anglin

Manufactured in the United States of America
First Printing: 1999 10,000
Second Printing: 2001 10,000

Contents

Professional Credits

HOWARD CRAIG PLOTKIN is a food stylist and creative consultant to the advertising industry. A native of McLean, Virginia, currently residing in Coral Springs, Florida, Howard has studied at American University, the Culinary Institute of America, and the National Gallery of Art. Working with such culinary icons as Wolfgang Puck, Julia Child, and Martha Stewart, Howard's stylings have been published in *Bon Appetit, Food and Wine,* and the *Chicago Tribune* (and its subsidiaries, including our own *Sun-Sentinel*), to name just a few.

ANDREW ITKOFF, a thirty-six-year-old resident of Plantation, grew up in Miami Beach, moving to Broward County two years ago with his wife Valerie and daughter Colby. "I was looking for a place to raise my children where I knew they'd be safe and have the childhood I had growing up in South Florida. The Fort Lauderdale area reminds me of Miami Beach twenty-five years ago."

With a bachelor's degree in fine arts from Florida International University, Andrew pursued a career in photojournalism. Having been a staff photographer at the *Hollywood Sun-Tattler, The Miami Review,* and the *Sun-Sentinel,* Andrew left newspaper photography to freelance. Having moved from the local to the national papers, such as *The New York Times, USA Today,* and *The Washington Post,* his business flourished. He currently is working primarily for magazines, which include *Time, Newsweek, Woman's World, Business Week,* and *People.*

This is Andrew's first cookbook project, although he is well acquainted with food photography, having photographed culinary dishes for many publications, including the 1998 and 1999 editions of *South Florida Fine Dining Guide.* "Completing this book has allowed me to accomplish a goal that gives me great satisfaction," Andrew says. "I thank the Junior League of Greater Fort Lauderdale for allowing me the opportunity to work with a wonderful group of individuals and achieve this goal."

Mission

The Junior League of Greater Fort Lauderdale, Inc. is a non-profit, tax-exempt organization of women committed to promoting voluntarism, developing the potential of women, and to improving the community through the effective action and leadership of trained volunteers. Its purpose is exclusively educational and charitable. The Junior League reaches out to women of all races, religions and national origins who demonstrate an interest in and commitment to voluntarism. The women of the Junior League share a feeling of responsibility toward their community and want to play a role in shaping its future.

Sponsored by

MR. AND MRS. WILLIAM JOHNSON

Prospectus

What the Junior League Does

The Junior League of Greater Fort Lauderdale was organized in 1937 as the Fort Lauderdale Junior Service League to provide the community with willing volunteers in civic and child welfare work. The first project was assisting Mrs. Parson's Day Nursery for working mothers, now known as Jack and Jill Nursery. In 1959, the Junior League of Greater Fort Lauderdale became a member of the Association of Junior Leagues International, an organization of 296 autonomous leagues throughout the United States, Canada, Great Britain and Mexico with 193,000 members.

The Junior League of Greater Fort Lauderdale has more than 800 active and sustaining members. Each year the League researches and initiates projects or expands services in response to community needs. Typically, projects are supported with financial, administrative and volunteer assistance until they become self-sufficient or responsibility is assumed by an appropriate agency. The Junior League of Greater Fort Lauderdale has been serving the Broward County community through numerous community projects since 1937.

How We Support Our Projects

The Junior League supports its projects through extensive volunteer time and expertise, as well as effective collaborations with other organizations in the community, solicitation of grants, community fund-raising events and fund development.

As a training organization committed to preparing women for effective lifelong volunteer service, the Junior League provides specific leadership development and skills training opportunities, as well as hands-on experience. The costs associated with our twofold purpose, training and community service, are met through membership dues and fund-raising activities.

Our membership dues and financial contributions more than cover all administrative costs of the organization; therefore, we can ensure that all financial support garnered through our fund development efforts are returned to the community. Our major sources of financial support include:

Junior League Thrift Shop—"Bloomin' Deals"
Riverwalk Run
Holiday Isles Market
"Chairs That Care" Gala
Made In The Shade Cookbook
Corporate and individual donations
Grants from various sources

A Glimpse at Our Legacy

Jack and Jill Nursery, established in 1942, is a comprehensive day-care center serving low-income families and ultimately assisting them in achieving self-sufficiency. The nursery provides an early-childhood learning program, nutritional meals and a loving environment for 120 children.

Henderson Mental Health Center, founded in 1953, is a private, nonprofit mental health facility. Organized into six diagnostic/treatment areas, the center serves the chronically mentally ill as well as treating individuals and families requiring intervention.

Museum of Art had its beginnings in 1958 in a renovated hardware store on Las Olas Boulevard. Today the museum is a nationally accredited fine arts institution housed in its own unique building in downtown Fort Lauderdale. Upon its opening, the Junior League committed financial resources and volunteers to provide an orientation gallery. In 1985, a multi-image program was established called Art Amaze, a hands-on gallery for audiences of all ages, with a special focus on children.

Volunteer Broward was formed in 1969 as a clearinghouse for recruiting and interviewing volunteers to match them with nonprofit agency positions. Volunteer Broward also offers workshops on effective management, leadership and volunteer program coordination.

King-Cromartie House, one of Fort Lauderdale's pioneer homes, was relocated and restored in 1971 to establish and ensure historic preservation in the community.

The Discovery Center, now the Museum of Discovery and Science, was founded in 1973 as a hands-on museum of art, science and history designed to encourage interaction and stimulation.

Kids in Distress, founded in 1976, is a comprehensive treatment program providing residential crisis care and a long-term therapeutic preschool program responding to children who have suffered from child abuse and neglect. The program also offers individual, family and group counseling to facilitate establishment of healthy family relationships for parents and children.

Partners in Education, which began in 1983, is a joint project with the Greater Fort Lauderdale Chamber of Commerce and the Broward County School Board designed to promote public education by pairing businesses and schools in mutually beneficial partnerships.

Too Good for Drugs (Me-ology) is a drug education program for public school fifth graders designed to create self awareness and provide information about drug and substance abuse. The program began in 1984 and includes training of community volunteers and school counselors.

Family Advocates: In 1991 trained Junior League counselors began working with expectant mothers to ensure that they can access timely prenatal care. Our partners include Healthy Mothers/Healthy Babies, the U.S. Public Health Department and the Florida Department of Health and Rehabilitative Services.

S.O.S. Children's Village, which opened in November 1992, is the first such village built in the United States. S.O.S. follows an internationally successful approach for providing permanent homes for hard-to-place children. The League provided support in education, public relations and grant writing, as well as matching a gift for furnishing the homes.

Susan B. Anthony Center: With a mission to help women with children continue their recovery from substance abuse, the League opened the Susan B. Anthony Center, a residential facility for women and children.

O.U.R. House stands for "offering unique reunifications." Since 1994, O.U.R. House has provided a neutral meeting place for supervised visits between parents and children who have been separated due to divorce, neglect or abusive relationships.

Family Living Center is a collaborative project between the League, Broward House and Children's Diagnostic and Treatment Center to provide housing for families where one or more of the members has HIV/AIDS. There is also an on-site Respite Child Care Center.

Don't Shake the Baby is a successful program in assisting community awareness and education in the prevention of Shaken Baby Syndrome and all child abuse.

Broward Partnership for the Homeless opened in 1999. It is a 200-bed facility for the homeless in Broward County. The League furnished and decorated a "Family Living Area" and made for a homelike and friendly environment.

CAPA-Cellular Aid to Prevent Abuse is a program to help abused women, reducing repeat domestic violence by giving victims a cellular phone that has been pre-programmed to dial only 911.

Our Current Community Projects

Junior League "Play Station" in Holiday Park: The Junior League of Greater Fort Lauderdale, in collaboration with the City of Fort Lauderdale, is building a signature playground facility within the refurbished Holiday Park Complex. The year 2000 marks the beginning of a four-year commitment by the League to raise $200,000 to build the train-themed playground. The playground will be fully ADA compliant, providing wheelchair access and special swings for young children with special needs. There will be age-appropriate play areas and extensive safety features, as well as family-friendly seating. In addition to the fund-raising efforts, the Junior League of Greater Fort Lauderdale will oversee the design of the playground, choose equipment and vendors, and approve landscaping within the playground area. Further, the League will facilitate the outreach efforts with potential park sponsors, efforts which may include grant writing, private donor solicitation and sponsorships of items used in the playground itself.

Ronald McDonald House: The Ronald McDonald House at Broward General Medical Center will be a home away from home for families who must travel many miles outside of their own communities to seek medical attention for a child. The Junior League of Greater Fort Lauderdale will collaborate on the project with McDonald's Corporation, Ronald McDonald Children's Charities, the Chris Evert Women and Children's Center at Broward General Medical Center and the North Broward Hospital District. There are numerous volunteer opportunities for our League, such as assisting with the fund-raising, decorating or supplying rooms, volunteer scheduling, food drives, etc.

Done in a Day (DIAD): Junior Leagues use DIAD projects across the country to allow members to come together to target short-term projects that can be completed in a single day. Past DIAD projects include:

- Henderson Mental Village—New Vistas Rainbow Villas received landscaping and beautification.
- S.O.S. Children's Village—Halloween party including costumes, refreshments and decorations.
- Kids in Distress—Miracle on 26th Street event for major contributors, assisted children in cookie baking project.

- Susan B. Anthony Center—Evening at the Christmas Pageant for 55 residents and Christmas Party.
- Jack and Jill Nursery—Clean-up day involving interior and exterior beautification.
- Positive Images—The committee collected suits and accessories from our members for welfare recipients entering into the job force.
- Special Olympics—Assisted athletes and served refreshments at the Summer Games.
- Spring into Reading—The committee has provided Headstart children with books and an afternoon of reading and refreshments in a joint effort with children from several different elementary schools.

Our Current Fund-Raisers

Made In The Shade: Junior League cookbooks have traditionally proven to be successful fund-raisers for Leagues across the country, highlighting regional flavors, gourmet presentations and family-friendly cuisine. Featuring over 250 recipes tested in local kitchens, *Made In The Shade* has proven to be a great success in both fund-raising efforts and community awareness for the Junior League of Greater Fort Lauderdale.

Thrift Shop: A major fund-raiser since its founding in 1940, the Junior League Thrift Shop "Bloomin' Deals" has served generations of Broward County citizens. Supported through donations from League members and the community, Bloomin' Deals has consistently won "The Best Thrift Shop in Broward County." Bloomin' Deals is located at 2031 Wilton Drive in Wilton Manors and serves an estimated 10,000 customers per year. Items not sold are donated to local shelters and church groups serving an even broader need.

Holiday Isles Market is a shopping extravaganza designed to kick off the holiday season in Fort Lauderdale. Local and national merchants showcase unique giftware, crafts and holiday items. Ten percent of all sales from the opening night go directly to the Junior League. With over 50 vendors, auction items and diverse raffle items, as well as special events throughout the weekend, Holiday Isles is a great opportunity to raise funds while having a good time.

Riverwalk Run is a new fund-raiser scheduled for March 2001. Olympian and National Champion Keith Brantley will lead the runners, walkers and strollers beginning at Riverwalk in downtown Fort Lauderdale. The race will proceed down Las Olas Boulevard, through the Poinsettia Heights neighborhood, and return to the city center. The League estimates that 1,000 runners and walkers will participate. Special events surrounding the run will include a dinner, children's entertainment and an awards ceremony at Riverwalk.

Chairs That Care Gala: In collaboration with the Young at Art Children's Museum and Ethan Allen Home Interiors, the Junior League of Greater Fort Lauderdale is participating in this special event. Celebrity artists, sports teams or individuals, performance troupes, singers, actors, etc., that have agreed to participate in this fund-raiser, are given a child-size chair to decorate for an auction that benefits the Junior League of Greater Fort Lauderdale and the Young at Art Children's Museum. Past chairs have been created by Romero Britto, Versace and Gloria Estefan and the Miami Heat, just to name a few.

JUST FOR STARTERS

APPETIZERS

BEVERAGES

SOUPS

Sponsored by

ANTIQUES & COUNTRY PINE

Artichoke Dip

1 cup grated Parmesan cheese
1 cup mayonnaise
1 (14-ounce) can artichoke hearts, drained, chopped
1 (8-ounce) can spinach, drained (optional)
½ cup chopped broccoli (optional)
½ cup chopped red bell pepper (optional)
½ cup grated Parmesan cheese
  Paprika to taste

Combine 1 cup cheese, mayonnaise and artichoke hearts in a bowl and mix well. Stir in the spinach, broccoli and red pepper. Spoon into a baking dish. Sprinkle with ½ cup cheese and paprika.

Bake at 350 degrees for 15 minutes or until brown and bubbly. Serve warm with sliced crusty French bread or assorted party crackers.

SERVES 6

Florida is named for the Spanish Easter Festival of Flowers.

Salsy Cilantro Salsa

8 to 10 plum tomatoes, chopped
½ red onion, chopped
1 bunch cilantro, finely chopped
  Juice of 2 limes
1 teaspoon minced garlic
½ habañero, seeded, finely minced
  Salt and pepper to taste

Combine the tomatoes, onion, cilantro, lime juice, garlic, habañero, salt and pepper in a bowl and mix well. Serve with tortilla chips. May substitute 1 jalapeño for the habañero.

SERVES 12 TO 15

Note: *Cut the habañeros with a knife and fork to avoid contact with the skin, or process in a food processor with the cilantro.*

OVERLEAF: *Gorgonzola-Stuffed Endive*

Mexican Corn Dip

3   (11-ounce) cans Mexicorn,
     drained
2   cups shredded Cheddar cheese
1   (4-ounce) can chopped green
     chiles
1   (4-ounce) can jalapeños, drained,
     chopped
1   cup mayonnaise
1   cup sour cream
     Tabasco sauce to taste
     Cayenne to taste
     Garlic powder to taste

Combine the corn, cheese, chiles and jalapeños in a bowl and mix well. Stir in a mixture of the mayonnaise and sour cream. Season with Tabasco sauce, cayenne and garlic powder. Chill, covered, until serving time. Serve with tortilla chips.

SERVES 6 TO 8

Curry Dip

¾   cup mayonnaise
1½   tablespoons grated onion
1½   tablespoons catsup
1½   tablespoons honey
1½   teaspoons fresh lemon juice
1½   teaspoons curry powder

Combine the mayonnaise, onion, catsup, honey, lemon juice and curry powder in a bowl and mix well. Chill, covered, for 8 to 10 hours. Serve with your favorite raw vegetables.

SERVES 6

Note: *Serve as a dressing over crab meat and avocado salad for a different twist.*

Tropical Guacamole Dip

1   red onion, cut into quarters
1   papaya, coarsely chopped
2   avocados, coarsely chopped
1   tomato, peeled, coarsely chopped
2   green onions, chopped
3   tablespoons chopped fresh
    cilantro
2   cloves of garlic, minced
$^1/_2$ Scotch bonnet pepper, minced
$^1/_4$ cup lime juice
1   tablespoon cumin
1   teaspoon hot pepper sauce
$^1/_8$ teaspoon salt
$^1/_8$ teaspoon pepper

Combine the onion, papaya, avocados, tomato, green onions, cilantro, garlic and pepper in a bowl and mix well. Add the lime juice, cumin, hot pepper sauce, salt and pepper and mix well.
   Serve with tortilla chips or plantain chips.

SERVES 10 TO 15

Florida has 5 percent of the 100 largest cities in the United States.

Pineapple Dip

$^1/_4$ cup (or more) chopped pecans
8   ounces cream cheese, softened
$^1/_2$ cup mayonnaise
1   (8-ounce) can crushed pineapple, drained

Spread the pecans on a baking sheet. Toast at 350 degrees until light brown, stirring occasionally. Let stand until cool.
   Beat the cream cheese and mayonnaise in a mixer bowl until creamy. Add the pecans and pineapple and mix well. Chill, covered, for 1 hour. Serve with assorted party crackers.

SERVES 5 TO 10

Mango Papaya Relish

2	large poblanos, seeded
1	large red bell pepper
1	large yellow bell pepper
1/2	large red onion
5	tablespoons olive oil
2	to 3 tablespoons chopped gingerroot
2	to 3 tablespoons chopped garlic
2	large ripe mangoes
2	medium ripe papayas
1/4	cup white wine vinegar
1/4	cup sour orange juice
1/4	cup lime juice
	Honey to taste
	Crème de coconut to taste
1	to 2 teaspoons cinnamon
1/8	teaspoon ground cloves
4	to 5 tablespoons chopped fresh cilantro

Cut the poblanos, red pepper, yellow pepper and onion into 1/8x1-inch strips. Sauté the vegetables in the olive oil in a skillet until tender and the onion is light brown. Stir in the gingerroot and garlic. Cook for several minutes.

Cut the mangoes and papayas into 1/2-inch pieces. Add to the pepper mixture and mix well. Sauté for several minutes. Deglaze the skillet with the wine vinegar, sour orange juice and lime juice, scraping up any browned bits. Add the honey and crème de coconut until you have a sweet and sour balance in the flavor. Stir in the cinnamon and cloves.

Cook over low heat until slightly thickened, tasting and adjusting the seasonings as desired and stirring frequently. The relish will thicken during the cooling process. Let stand until cool. Stir in the cilantro.

SERVES 20

Mediterranean-Style Tomato Dip

1	(15-ounce) can garbanzo beans, drained, rinsed
1	(8-ounce) can tomato sauce
1/2	cup plain nonfat yogurt
2	tablespoons minced fresh cilantro
2	tablespoons minced green onions
1 1/2	teaspoons garlic powder
1	teaspoon prepared horseradish
1	teaspoon cumin

Process the beans, tomato sauce, yogurt and cilantro in a food processor just until smooth. Combine the mixture with the green onions, garlic powder, horseradish and cumin in a bowl and mix well.

Chill, covered, for several hours to allow the flavors to marry. Serve with pita chips or raw vegetables.

MAKES 2 CUPS

Caramelized Brie

1	**large round Brie cheese**
1	**cup packed brown sugar**
¹/₂	**cup butter**
1	**cup pecan halves**

Remove the top rind of the Brie. Place the round on a baking sheet. Combine the brown sugar and butter in a saucepan. Cook until the butter melts, stirring frequently. Stir in the pecans.

Spread the pecan mixture over the top of the Brie. Bake at 325 degrees for 45 minutes. Serve warm with water crackers and sliced apples.

SERVES 10

Crab Meat Mousse

1	**(10-ounce) can cream of shrimp soup**
6	**ounces cream cheese**
¹/₄	**cup minced onion**
1	**cup mayonnaise**
2	**envelopes unflavored gelatin**
1	**cup cold water**
1	**pound fresh or canned crab meat**
1	**cup minced celery**

Combine the soup, cream cheese and onion in a saucepan. Cook over low heat until the cream cheese melts, stirring constantly. Remove from heat. Stir in the mayonnaise.

Sprinkle the gelatin over the cold water in a saucepan. Let stand until softened. Heat the gelatin mixture over medium heat until the gelatin dissolves, stirring constantly. Stir into the soup mixture. Fold in the crab meat and celery.

Spoon into a greased 6-cup mold. Chill for 4 hours or longer. Serve with assorted party crackers.

SERVES 8

Garlic Feta Cheese Spread

1   **clove of garlic, minced**

¼   **teaspoon salt**

12   **ounces cream cheese, chopped, softened**

8   **ounces feta cheese, crumbled**

½   **cup mayonnaise**

¼   **teaspoon marjoram, crushed**

¼   **teaspoon dillweed, crushed**

¼   **teaspoon thyme, crushed**

¼   **teaspoon basil, crushed**

Mix the garlic and salt in a bowl until of a pasty consistency. Process the garlic mixture, cream cheese, feta cheese, mayonnaise, marjoram, dillweed, thyme and basil in a food processor until of the desired consistency. Spoon into a crock.

Chill, covered, for 2 hours. Serve with assorted party crackers. May store in the refrigerator for up to 1 week.

MAKES 1½ CUPS

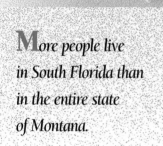

More people live in South Florida than in the entire state of Montana.

Pesto and Sun-Dried Tomato Spread

¼   **cup chopped sun-dried tomatoes**

¼   **cup pesto**

1   **cup whipped cream cheese**

Line a small bowl with plastic wrap. Sprinkle 1 teaspoon of the tomatoes over the bottom. Spread with some of the pesto. Layer the cream cheese to measure ½ inch over the prepared layers. Repeat the layering process until all of the ingredients are used, ending with the cream cheese.

Chill, covered, for 12 to 24 hours. Invert onto a serving platter. Serve with assorted party crackers.

SERVES 6 TO 8

Smoked Salmon Spread

1   cup ricotta cheese

2   ounces smoked salmon, chopped

2   tablespoons chopped fresh
     dillweed

2   tablespoons drained capers

2   teaspoons lemon juice

2   teaspoons catsup

1   teaspoon horseradish
     Salt and pepper to taste

Process the ricotta cheese in a food processor or blender until puréed. Add the salmon, dillweed, capers, lemon juice, catsup and horseradish. Process just until mixed. Season with salt and pepper.

Store, covered, in the refrigerator until serving time. Serve with assorted party crackers.

MAKES 1⅓ CUPS

Baked Brie Bread

1   loaf French bread

4   ounces pesto

3   tablespoons balsamic vinegar

3   roasted red peppers, julienned
     Brie cheese, sliced

Cut the loaf lengthwise into halves. Spread the pesto over the cut sides of the bread. Drizzle with the balsamic vinegar. Layer the red peppers and enough cheese to cover over 1 bread half. Top with the remaining bread half. Wrap in foil.

Bake at 350 degrees for 45 minutes or until heated through. Cut into 1-inch slices. Serve warm.

SERVES 6 TO 8

Caribbean Cashew-Encrusted and Coconut Jerk Seafood Rolls

1	pound scallops, coarsely chopped
1	pound shrimp, peeled, deveined, coarsely chopped
2	large poblanos, seeded, finely chopped
1	large yellow bell pepper, finely chopped
1	large red bell pepper, finely chopped
½	large red onion, finely chopped
5	tablespoons olive oil
¼	cup chopped gingerroot
¼	cup chopped garlic
	Salt and pepper to taste
¾	cup white wine
	Juice 3 limes
	Jamaican Jerk seasoning to taste
½	bunch green onions, finely chopped
¼	cup chopped fresh cilantro
	Zest of 3 limes
16	to 20 spring roll wrappers
1	egg, beaten
2	cups flour
4	eggs, beaten
2	cups shredded coconut
2	cups chopped cashews
	Vegetable oil for deep-frying
	Mango Papaya Relish (page 15)
	Sprigs of watercress

Process ⅓ of the scallops and ⅓ of the shrimp separately in a food processor just until puréed. Sauté the poblanos, bell peppers and onion in the olive oil in a skillet until tender and the onion is light brown. Stir in the gingerroot and garlic. Cook for 30 seconds. Season with salt and pepper. Stir in the white wine, lime juice and Jamaican Jerk seasoning. Cook until reduced to a syrupy consistency, stirring frequently. Let stand until cool.

Combine the syrup mixture with the remaining chopped shrimp, shrimp purée, remaining chopped scallops, scallop purée, green onions, cilantro and lime zest. Taste and adjust seasonings with salt, pepper and Jamaican Jerk seasoning.

Lay the spring roll wrappers 1 at a time on a hard surface. Spoon about 2 ounces of the shrimp mixture in the center of each wrapper. Roll each halfway and fold in the edges. Fold to the end. Brush the end with 1 beaten egg to seal. Freeze in the freezer.

Coat the rolls with the flour. Dip in 4 beaten eggs in a shallow dish. Coat with the coconut and cashews. Fry in 350- to 360-degree oil in a deep fat fryer until golden brown; drain. Place on a baking sheet. Bake at 375 degrees until cooked through; drain.

Cut the ends off the hot spring rolls. Cut each roll into halves on the bias so it can stand on the plate like a piece of sushi. Serve each roll with 2 tablespoons of Mango Papaya Relish and top with a sprig of fresh watercress.

MAKES 16 TO 20 ROLLS

Chicken Crescent Bundles

3   ounces cream cheese, softened
2   tablespoons melted margarine
2   cups chopped cooked chicken
2   tablespoons milk
1   tablespoon chopped chives or onion
1   tablespoon chopped pimento
¼   teaspoon salt
⅛   teaspoon pepper
2   (8-count) cans crescent rolls
     Melted margarine
¾   cup crushed seasoned croutons

Mix the cream cheese and 2 tablespoons margarine in a bowl until smooth. Stir in the chicken, milk, chives, pimento, salt and pepper.

Unroll the crescent roll dough. Separate into 8 rectangles and seal perforations. Spoon ¼ cup of the chicken mixture in the center of each rectangle. Pull the 4 corners of each rectangle to the center and twist to seal.

Brush the bundles with melted margarine. Coat with the croutons. Arrange the bundles on an ungreased baking sheet. Bake at 350 degrees for 15 to 20 minutes or until light brown.

MAKES 8 BUNDLES

Sweet and Easy Chicken Wings

4   pounds chicken wings
1   (5-ounce) bottle soy sauce
1   (1-pound) package brown sugar

Separate the chicken wings at the joints, discarding the tips. Arrange in a single layer in a baking dish.

Mix the soy sauce and brown sugar in a bowl. Pour over the chicken. Bake, covered, at 300 degrees for 3 hours, turning once.

SERVES 12

Conch Fritters

1¼ **pounds conch**

8 **slices white bread, cut into ¹/₂-inch cubes**

¹/₂ **large onion, chopped**

2 **eggs**

2 **tablespoons Tabasco sauce**

2 **tablespoons lime juice**

1 **teaspoon dry mustard**

¹/₄ **teaspoon salt**

¹/₄ **teaspoon freshly ground pepper**

¹/₄ **teaspoon thyme**

1 **clove of garlic, minced**

1¹/₂ **cups cracker meal**

Vegetable oil for deep-frying

Cocktail Sauce

Cut the orange fin and foot from the conch and discard. Chop the conch. Combine the conch, bread, onion, eggs, Tabasco sauce, lime juice, dry mustard, salt, pepper, thyme and garlic in a food processor container or grinder.

Process until ground. Shape into 1½- to 2-inch balls with moist hands. Coat with the cracker meal. Heat the oil in a deep fat fryer to 350 degrees. Fry the fritters in batches in the hot oil for 5 minutes or until golden brown; drain. Serve with the Cocktail Sauce.

MAKES 30 FRITTERS

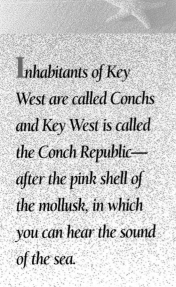

Inhabitants of Key West are called Conchs and Key West is called the Conch Republic— after the pink shell of the mollusk, in which you can hear the sound of the sea.

Cocktail Sauce

2 **cups catsup**

2 **tablespoons horseradish**

Combine the catsup and horseradish in a bowl and mix well. Taste and add additional horseradish if desired.

Crostini with Tomatoes

1   **baguette French bread, cut into 12 (¼-inch) slices**
¾   **cup chopped Roma tomatoes**
¼   **cup chopped drained oil-packed sun-dried tomatoes**
2   **tablespoons chopped fresh basil**
3½   **ounces goat cheese, cut into 12 thin slices**
     Pepper to taste

Arrange the bread slices in a single layer on a baking sheet. Bake at 350 degrees for 5 minutes or until light brown on 1 side. Combine the tomatoes, sun-dried tomatoes and basil in a bowl and mix well.

Place 1 slice of the goat cheese on each bread slice. Top each with some of the tomato mixture. Sprinkle generously with the pepper. Bake for 3 to 5 minutes. Serve immediately.

MAKES 12 CROSTINI

Crab Won Tons

8   **ounces cream cheese, softened**
¼   **cup grated Parmesan cheese**
¼   **cup shredded crab meat**
1   **tablespoon mayonnaise**
1½   **teaspoons garlic powder**
     Chopped green onions to taste
     Won ton wrappers
     Vegetable oil for deep-frying
     Hot Plum Sauce

Beat the cream cheese in a mixer bowl until creamy. Stir in the Parmesan cheese, crab meat, mayonnaise, garlic powder and green onions. Spoon 1 to 2 teaspoons of the mixture onto each won ton wrapper. Twist to seal. Fry the won tons in hot oil in a deep fat fryer until golden brown; drain. Serve with Hot Plum Sauce.

SERVES 10

Hot Plum Sauce

½   **cup plum jam**
2   **tablespoons vinegar**
2   **tablespoons catsup**
2   **tablespoons brown sugar**

Mix the jam, vinegar, catsup and brown sugar in a microwave-safe dish. Microwave for 30 seconds and stir.

Stuffed French Bread

16   ounces cream cheese, softened
2   (4-ounce) cans chopped clams,
      drained
½   cup chopped fresh parsley
½   cup minced green onions
2   tablespoons lemon juice
1   tablespoon Worcestershire sauce
1   teaspoon salt
½   teaspoon hot pepper sauce
2   round loaves French bread

Beat the cream cheese in a mixer bowl until creamy. Stir in the clams, parsley, green onions, lemon juice, Worcestershire sauce, salt and hot pepper sauce.

Cut the top from 1 bread loaf and reserve. Remove the center of bottom part carefully, leaving a shell and reserve. Spoon the cream cheese mixture into the shell. Replace the top and wrap with foil. Bake at 250 degrees for 3 hours.

Cut the reserved bread center and remaining loaf into cubes. Place the loaf on a serving platter and arrange the bread cubes around the loaf.

SERVES 10 TO 12

Note: *Wrap with a plaid ribbon for a great look for a Christmas party—a pretty, edible package. Change the color of the ribbon, or add an American flag, valentines, or whatever to make it a hit at any celebration.*

Gorgonzola-Stuffed Endive

¼   cup butter
1   pound walnuts, coarsely chopped
½   cup packed brown sugar
9   heads endive, separated into
      spears
1   pound gorgonzola, crumbled
      Balsamic vinegar
      Italian salad dressing
1   red bell pepper, finely chopped
1   yellow bell pepper, finely chopped
      Salad greens

Heat the butter in a skillet until melted. Add the walnuts, tossing to coat. Stir in the brown sugar. Cook for 10 minutes or until caramelized, stirring constantly. Remove the walnuts with a slotted spoon to paper towels. Let stand until cool.

Spoon the walnuts onto the endive spears. Top with the cheese. Drizzle with a mixture of equal parts balsamic vinegar and your favorite Italian salad dressing; do not use creamy Italian. Sprinkle with the red and yellow peppers. Arrange the endive spears on a platter lined with salad greens.

SERVES 50

Photograph for this recipe appears on page 10.

Key West's cemetery, which fills twenty-one prime acres in the heart of the island's historic district, is the site of some quirky headstones. "I Told You I Was Sick" reads one of a hypochondriacal lady, while close by is "Call Me For Dinner."

Green Chile Tortilla Pinwheels

8	ounces cream cheese, softened
1	(4-ounce) can chopped green chiles, drained
2	tablespoons picante sauce
¼	teaspoon garlic salt
3	or 4 large flour tortillas

Beat the cream cheese in a mixer bowl until creamy. Stir in the chiles, picante sauce and garlic salt. Spread the cream cheese mixture over the tortillas. Roll tightly to enclose the filling.

Wrap the tortillas individually in plastic wrap. Chill until serving time.

Cut each tortilla roll into ½-inch slices just before serving. Serve with additional picante sauce.

SERVES 10

Hot Mushroom Turnovers

8   ounces cream cheese, softened
$1/2$ cup butter or margarine, softened
$1\frac{3}{4}$ cups flour
3   tablespoons butter or margarine
8   ounces fresh mushrooms, minced
1   large onion, minced
$1/2$ cup sour cream
2   tablespoons flour
1   teaspoon salt
$1/4$ teaspoon thyme
1   egg, lightly beaten

Combine the cream cheese and $1/2$ cup butter in a mixer bowl. Beat at medium speed until creamy, scraping the bowl occasionally. Add $1\frac{3}{4}$ cups flour gradually, beating until blended. Divide the dough into 2 portions. Shape each portion into a ball. Chill, covered, for 1 hour.

Heat 3 tablespoons butter in a skillet until melted. Stir in the mushrooms and onion. Sauté until tender. Stir in the sour cream, 2 tablespoons flour, salt and thyme. Remove from heat.

Roll 1 dough portion $1/8$ inch thick on a lightly floured surface. Cut with a $2\frac{1}{2}$-inch round cutter. Place the rounds on a greased baking sheet. Repeat the process with the remaining dough portion.

Spoon 1 teaspoon of the mushroom mixture onto half of each round. Brush the edges with the egg. Fold over to enclose the filling. Press the edges with a fork to seal; prick the tops with a fork. Brush with the egg. Bake at 450 degrees for 8 to 10 minutes or until golden brown.

MAKES $3\frac{1}{2}$ DOZEN TURNOVERS

Spicy Stuffed Mushrooms

8   ounces spicy pork sausage
25   medium to large fresh mushrooms
8   ounces cream cheese, softened

Brown the sausage in a skillet, stirring until crumbly; drain. Remove the stems from the mushrooms and chop, keeping the caps intact.

Beat the cream cheese in a mixer bowl until creamy. Stir in the sausage and chopped mushroom stems. Spoon about 1 teaspoon of the mixture into each mushroom cap. Arrange on an ungreased baking sheet. Broil for 5 minutes or until golden brown and bubbly.

SERVES 10 TO 12

25

Hot Olive Cheese Puffs

1   **cup shredded sharp Cheddar cheese**

$1/2$ **cup flour**

3   **tablespoons butter, softened**

$1/2$ **teaspoon salt**

$1/2$ **teaspoon paprika**

    Pimento-stuffed green olives, drained

Combine the cheese, flour, butter, salt and paprika in a bowl and mix well. Shape the dough around the olives to enclose. Arrange on an ungreased baking sheet. Bake at 400 degrees for 15 minutes.

SERVES 8 TO 10

Note: *May be prepared in advance, unbaked, and chilled or frozen until just before baking.*

Butterfly World in Coconut Creek houses one of the world's largest butterfly collections.

Italian Sausage Bread

2   loaves frozen bread dough

12 ounces sweet Italian sausage

12 ounces hot Italian sausage

16 ounces mushrooms, sliced

1   medium yellow onion, sliced, separated into rings

2   cups shredded mozzarella cheese

2/3 cup grated Parmesan cheese

Thaw the bread dough and let rise using package directions. Brown the sausage with the mushrooms and onion in a skillet, stirring until the sausage is crumbly and the vegetables are tender; drain.

Roll 1 bread loaf 1/4 inch thick on a lightly floured surface. Spread with half the sausage mixture. Sprinkle with 1 cup of the mozzarella cheese and 1/3 cup of the Parmesan cheese. Roll to enclose the filling. Fold the ends under to form a loaf. Place in a greased loaf pan. Repeat the process with the remaining bread loaf, remaining sausage mixture, remaining mozzarella cheese and remaining Parmesan cheese.

Bake at 350 degrees for 30 to 40 minutes or until a wooden pick inserted in the center comes out clean. Remove to a serving plate. Cut into slices. Serve with warm tomato sauce if desired.

SERVES 12

Margarita Shrimp

1   pound medium shrimp, peeled, deveined

5   tablespoons corn oil

1/2 cup minced green onions

2   large cloves of garlic, minced

1/4 cup tequila

2   tablespoons fresh lime juice

1/2 teaspoon coarse salt
    Lime wedges

Cut the shrimp lengthwise into halves. Heat the corn oil in a skillet over medium-high heat until hot. Add the shrimp, green onions and garlic. Sauté for 1 minute or until the shrimp turn pink. Remove from heat. Stir in the tequila.

Bring to a boil, stirring to scrap any browned bits. Transfer the shrimp mixture to a serving bowl. Let stand until cool. Add the lime juice and salt, tossing to coat. Top with lime wedges.

SERVES 6

Note: *May be prepared up to 6 hours in advance and stored, covered with plastic wrap, in the refrigerator.*

Tomato Basil Tart

1   **all ready pie pastry**
½   **cup shredded mozzarella cheese**
4   **or 5 plum tomatoes, sliced, drained**
1½ **cups shredded mozzarella cheese**
1   **cup chopped fresh basil**
½   **cup mayonnaise**
¼   **cup freshly grated Parmesan cheese**
4   **cloves of garlic, minced**

Fit the pastry over the bottom and up the side of a quiche dish. Sprinkle with ½ cup mozzarella cheese. Arrange the tomato slices over the cheese.

Mix 1½ cups mozzarella cheese, basil, mayonnaise, Parmesan cheese and garlic in a bowl. Spread over the prepared layers. Bake at 375 degrees for 25 to 30 minutes.

SERVES 8 TO 10

Note: *Reduce those fat grams by using nonfat mayonnaise and part-skim mozzarella cheese.*

Veggie Bites

2   **(8-count) cans crescent rolls**
1   **egg, beaten**
16 **ounces cream cheese, softened**
1   **cup mayonnaise**
1   **envelope ranch salad dressing mix**
¾   **cup shredded Cheddar cheese**
½   **cup finely chopped broccoli**
½   **cup finely chopped cauliflower**
½   **cup finely chopped mushrooms**
½   **cup finely chopped green bell pepper**
½   **cup finely chopped tomato**

Unroll the roll dough. Separate into rectangles. Spread over the bottom of an ungreased 9x13-inch baking pan, pressing edges and perforations to seal. Brush with the egg. Bake at 375 degrees for 11 to 13 minutes or until light brown. Let stand until cool.

Beat the cream cheese, mayonnaise and dressing mix in a mixer bowl until creamy. Spread over the baked layer. Sprinkle with the Cheddar cheese, broccoli, cauliflower, mushrooms, green pepper and tomato. Chill for 2 hours. Cut into 1-inch squares.

MAKES 8 DOZEN SQUARES

Florida Amaretto Sours

1   (6-ounce) can frozen pink
     lemonade concentrate
1   lemonade can amaretto
1   lemonade can water
8   to 12 ice cubes

Combine the lemonade concentrate, amaretto, water and ice cubes in a blender container. Process at high speed until slushy. Serve immediately.

SERVES 4

The state flower is the orange blossom, and the state beverage is (what else?) orange juice.

Sunny Champagne Sipper

1   quart pineapple sherbet, softened
4   cups orange juice, chilled
4   cups white grape juice, chilled
1   bottle Champagne, chilled
1   to 2 oranges, sliced
     Sprigs of mint

Spread the sherbet in ice cube trays or scoop with a melon baller. Refreeze for 8 to 10 hours. Combine the orange juice and grape juice in a large container. Add the Champagne just before serving and stir gently.

Place several sherbet cubes or balls in tall glasses. Add the Champagne mixture. Top each serving with an orange slice and/or a mint sprig.

SERVES 10 TO 12

Note: *This refreshing drink can be adapted to serve one or as many as you desire, using equal parts juice and Champagne.*

Citrus Surprise

1   (64-ounce) jar cranberry juice
1   (12-ounce) can frozen orange juice
     concentrate
1   (6-ounce) can frozen lemonade
     concentrate
1   fifth vodka
1   liter bottle lemon lime soda
     Orange or lemon slices

Combine the cranberry juice, orange juice concentrate, lemonade concentrate and vodka in a large freezer container and mix well. Freeze for 24 hours, stirring twice.

To serve, scoop the desired amount of the slushy mixture into each glass. Add an equal part of the lemon lime soda. Top each serving with an orange or lemon slice.

SERVES 15 TO 20

Note: *Don't let this slush punch sneak up on you. The alcohol is hidden by the tangy sweetness of the juices.*

Coffee Punch

1   gallon whole milk
1   (16-ounce) can chocolate syrup
1   cup instant coffee granules
2   (1/2-gallon) containers vanilla ice
     cream

Combine 1 to 2 cups of the milk, chocolate syrup and coffee granules in a saucepan. Cook over low heat until blended, stirring frequently. Combine with the remaining milk in a large container. Chill for 8 to 10 hours or until cold.

Cut the ice cream into small chunks and place in a punch bowl. Pour the milk mixture over the ice cream. Ladle into punch cups.

SERVES 16 TO 20

Cinnamon Coffee

10 cups water
4 cinnamon sticks
1 tablespoon (heaping) brown sugar
1 cup ground coffee
1 teaspoon ground cinnamon

Pour the water into a drip coffeemaker. Place the cinnamon stick and brown sugar in the glass container. Place the coffee and ground cinnamon in the brew basket. Brew using manufacturers' directions; stir. Pour into mugs. Serve with chocolate-almond dipped spoons.

SERVES 10

Note: *The flavor of the coffee is enhanced if allowed to stand before serving. The longer it stands, the richer the flavor.*

Tropical Melon Daiquiri

4 cups watermelon cubes, seeded
1/2 cup rum or vodka
1/4 cup Grand Marnier
2 tablespoons lime juice
2 tablespoons lemon juice
Crushed ice
Lime slices
Salt to taste (optional)

Freeze the watermelon, covered, for 6 hours or longer. Process the watermelon, rum, Grand Marnier, lime juice and lemon juice in a blender until smooth. Add enough crushed ice to measure 5 cups total beverage. Process until smooth.

Rub the rims of several wide-mouthed glasses with lime slices. Spread some salt in saucer. Spin the rim of each glass in salt. Pour the slushy mixture into the glasses. Top each glass with a lime slice.

SERVES 2 TO 4

Frozen Strawberry Daiquiri

1   (10-ounce) package frozen
    strawberries
1   (6-ounce) can frozen pink
    lemonade concentrate
1   (6-ounce) can frozen limeade
    concentrate
1   fifth white rum
6   lemonade cans water

Process the strawberries in a food processor until puréed. Combine the strawberry purée, lemonade concentrate, limeade concentrate, rum and water in a freezer container and mix well. Freeze until set, stirring every 30 minutes. Spoon into individual glasses or store in the freezer for future use.

SERVES 8

Gilchrest's Holiday Eggnog

2   cups brandy
1   cup rye whiskey
½   cup sherry
12   egg yolks
¾   cup sugar
4   cups milk
4   cups cream
12   egg whites

Combine the brandy, whiskey and sherry in a bowl and mix well. Beat the egg yolks in a mixer bowl until blended. Add the sugar and mix well. Add the brandy mixture 1 drop at a time, beating constantly at low speed. Add the milk and cream, beating constantly at low speed.

Beat the egg whites in a mixer bowl until stiff peaks form. Fold into the brandy mixture. Chill, covered, for several days before serving, stirring occasionally.

SERVES 15 TO 20

Frozen Margaritas

1   (6-ounce) can frozen limeade concentrate

²/₃ limeade can tequila

¹/₂ to ³/₄ limeade can water

¹/₂ limeade can Triple Sec

Sugar to taste

Ice

Combine the limeade concentrate, tequila, water, Triple Sec, sugar and the desired amount of ice in a food processor or blender container. Process until smooth. Spoon into a freezer container. Freeze until set.

SERVES 4

The "Orange Blossom Special" is not the name of a specific drink, but of the first Seaboard Air Line train to come through Fort Lauderdale in 1927.

Fort Lauderdale Sangria

¹/₂ gallon full-bodied red wine

1   (6-ounce) can frozen lemonade concentrate

1   orange, sliced

1   Key lime, sliced

¹/₂ mango, sliced

1   banana, sliced

1   cup grape halves

¹/₂ cup pineapple chunks

Combine the red wine, lemonade concentrate, orange slices, Key lime slices, mango, banana, grapes and pineapple in a container and mix well. Chill, covered, for 1 hour or longer.

SERVES 12 TO 15

Orange Mint Tea

4	**family tea bags**
8	**large mint leaves**
3	**cups boiling water**
6	**cups cold water**
1	**cup orange juice**
1	**cup sugar**
1/4	**cup lemon juice**
1	**orange, sliced**
4	**large mint leaves**

Combine the tea bags and 8 mint leaves with the boiling water in a saucepan. Steep for several minutes. Discard the tea bags and mint. Combine the tea, cold water, orange juice, sugar and lemon juice in a pitcher and mix well. Add the orange slices and 4 mint leaves. Serve over ice in individual glasses.

SERVES 8 TO 10

Winter Wassail

3	**large cooking apples, cored**
1	**tablespoon butter**
1	**teaspoon ground cinnamon**
1	**(64-ounce) jar apple cider**
6	**whole cloves**
6	**whole allspice**
2	**teaspoons nutmeg**
1	**(6-ounce) can frozen orange juice concentrate**
1	**(6-ounce) can frozen lemonade concentrate**
1	**cup packed brown sugar**
2	**oranges, sliced**
	Cinnamon sticks

Cut the apples into halves. Spread the cut sides with the butter and sprinkle with the ground cinnamon. Place the apples cut side down in a 9x13-inch baking dish. Bake at 350 degrees for 25 minutes or until tender.

Combine 2 cups of the apple cider, cloves, allspice and nutmeg in a 6-quart stockpot. Simmer over low heat for 10 minutes. Add the remaining apple cider, orange juice concentrate, lemonade concentrate and brown sugar and mix well. Cook until heated through; do not boil.

Pour the punch into a heated punch bowl. Add the apples and oranges. Serve warm with cinnamon sticks.

SERVES 12

Vodka Barrel Punch

1½ gallons citrus fruit punch

2 to 3 cups vodka, or to taste

2 cups orange juice

2 cups pineapple juice

1 cup grapefruit juice

½ cup lime juice

Orange, grapefruit, lemon and lime slices

Combine the fruit punch, vodka, orange juice, pineapple juice, grapefruit juice and lime juice in a large container and mix well. Add the orange slices, grapefruit slices, lemon slices and lime slices. Chill for 3 to 4 hours before serving in a punch bowl. Ladle into punch cups.

SERVES 40

Wheat Berry, Feta and Grape Tomato Salad

2 cups wheat berries

4 cups water

1 bulb garlic

8 ounces feta cheese, crumbled

2 pints grape or cherry tomatoes, cut into halves

5 scallion bulbs with 2 inches tops, sliced

1 yellow bell pepper, chopped

2 carrots, chopped

1 seedless cucumber, chopped

½ cup pine nuts, toasted

½ cup snipped fresh basil

¼ cup chopped fresh parsley

1 cup fat-free balsamic vinaigrette

¼ cup balsamic vinegar

2 tablespoons grainy Dijon mustard

½ teaspoon salt

¼ teaspoon pepper

Combine the wheat berries with enough cold water to cover in a bowl. Soak for 8 to 10 hours; drain. Combine the wheat berries and 4 cups water in a saucepan. Bring to a boil; reduce heat to medium-low. Simmer, covered, for 1½ hours or until the wheat berry grains burst open and are tender, adding additional water as needed; drain.

Separate the garlic bulb into cloves and peel. Spray the garlic cloves with olive oil. Arrange in a baking pan. Roast at 400 degrees for 10 to 15 minutes or just until brown. Cool and coarsely chop. Combine the wheat berries, garlic, feta cheese, grape tomatoes, scallions, yellow pepper, carrots, cucumber, pine nuts, basil and parsley in a bowl and mix gently. Add a mixture of the balsamic vinaigrette, balsamic vinegar, Dijon mustard, salt and pepper and toss to mix. Chill, covered, until serving time. Keeps for several days.

SERVES 6 TO 8

Note: *May substitute a mixture of ¾ cup olive oil and ¼ cup balsamic vinegar for the fat-free balsamic vinaigrette.*

Chilled Avocado Soup

5   **ripe avocados, coarsely chopped**
      Juice of 2 limes
4   **cups buttermilk**
2   **cups chicken stock**
1¹/₂   **cups plain yogurt**
1   **teaspoon chili powder**
1   **clove of garlic, minced**
1   **teaspoon cumin**
¹/₈   **teaspoon cayenne**
¹/₈   **teaspoon mint**
3   **cucumbers, peeled, seeded, chopped**
      Salt to taste
¹/₄   **cup chopped fresh cilantro**

Process the avocados and lime juice in a blender until smooth. Pour into a bowl. Whisk in the buttermilk, stock and yogurt until blended. Stir in the chili powder, garlic, cumin, cayenne and mint. Add the cucumbers and mix gently. Season with salt. Ladle into soup bowls. Top each serving with cilantro.

SERVES 12

Carrot Vichyssoise

6   **cups chicken broth**
4   **cups chopped potatoes**
4   **cups chopped carrots**
2   **cups chopped leeks**
2   **teaspoons chicken bouillon granules**
2   **cups light cream**
¹/₂   **teaspoon salt**
¹/₂   **teaspoon white pepper**
3   **tablespoons grated carrot**
      Dillweed and/or minced chives

Combine the broth, potatoes, carrots, leeks and bouillon granules in a saucepan. Bring to a boil; reduce heat. Simmer, covered, for 10 minutes or until the vegetables are tender, stirring occasionally.

Process the broth mixture in a blender until smooth. Pour into a bowl. Whisk in the cream, salt and white pepper. Chill, covered, until serving time. Adjust seasonings. Ladle into chilled soup bowls. Top each serving with grated carrot and dillweed and/or chives.

SERVES 6 TO 10

Lobster Gazpacho

4	or 5 tomatoes
2	cucumbers, peeled, seeded
1	yellow onion
3	ribs celery
1	yellow bell pepper
$1/2$	cup red wine vinegar
$1/4$	cup olive oil
1	clove of garlic, crushed
	Tabasco sauce to taste
	Salt and pepper to taste
2	(12-ounce) cans vegetable juice cocktail
$1/3$	cup chopped fresh cilantro
2	Florida lobster tails, steamed

Blanch the tomatoes in boiling water in a saucepan for 15 seconds. Transfer the tomatoes to a bowl of ice water to cool. Peel, seed and chop the tomatoes. Chop the cucumbers, onion, celery and yellow pepper in various sizes.

Combine the tomatoes with the chopped vegetables in a bowl and mix well. Process 1/4 of the vegetable mixture in a blender or food processor until smooth. Stir the processed mixture into the chopped vegetables.

Whisk the wine vinegar and olive oil in a bowl. Stir in the garlic, Tabasco sauce, salt and pepper. Add to the vegetable mixture and mix well. Stir in the vegetable juice cocktail and cilantro. Chill, covered, in the refrigerator.

Remove the meat from the lobster tails and chop. Ladle the vegetable mixture into soup bowls. Add a portion of the lobster meat to each bowl just before serving.

SERVES 4 TO 6

Fort Lauderdale is home to the International Swimming Hall of Fame. Founded in 1965, the first name to enter the Hall of Fame was Johnny Weissmuller, Olympic gold medalist and "Tarzan" of movie fame.

Fruit Soup

6   tablespoons tapioca

5   cups water

⅔   cup sugar

⅛   teaspoon salt

1   (12-ounce) can frozen orange juice concentrate

1   pint sliced frozen peaches

2   (11-ounce) cans mandarin oranges, drained

1   (16-ounce) package frozen strawberries

1   (16-ounce) can grapefruit sections

2   or 3 bananas, sliced

Prepare the tapioca using package directions. Stir 2½ cups of the water, sugar and salt into the tapioca. Bring to a boil. Stir in the remaining 2½ cups water, orange juice concentrate, peaches, oranges, undrained strawberries, undrained grapefruit and bananas. Chill, covered, for 2 hours. Ladle into soup bowls.

SERVES 8

Pumpkin Soup

1   cup chopped onion

1   clove of garlic, minced

¼   cup butter

1   teaspoon curry powder

½   teaspoon salt

⅛   to ¼ teaspoon coriander

⅛   teaspoon red pepper flakes

3   cups chicken stock

1   (16-ounce) can pumpkin

1   cup half-and-half

Sauté the onion and garlic in the butter in a saucepan until tender. Stir in the curry powder, salt, coriander and red pepper flakes. Cook for 1 minute, stirring constantly. Add the stock and mix well.

Boil gently for 15 to 20 minutes, stirring frequently. Stir in the pumpkin and half-and-half. Cook for 5 minutes longer, stirring occasionally. Remove from heat. Let stand for 1 hour.

Process the pumpkin mixture in a blender until puréed. Ladle into soup bowls.

SERVES 6 TO 8

Black Bean Soup

2	pounds dried black turtle beans
3	cups chopped onions
8	cloves of garlic, crushed
1	cup olive oil
6	quarts water
1	meaty ham bone or smoked ham hock
2	tablespoons cumin
2	tablespoons chopped fresh parsley
1	tablespoon each oregano and salt
2	teaspoons black pepper
1	teaspoon cayenne
3	bay leaves
1/4	cup chopped fresh parsley
1	tablespoon each brown sugar and lemon juice
1	teaspoon cumin
	Chopped onions to taste
	Sour cream to taste

Sort and rinse the beans. Combine the beans with enough water to cover in a bowl. Let stand for 8 to 10 hours; drain.

Sauté 3 cups onions and garlic in the olive oil in a stockpot until tender. Add the beans, 6 quarts water and ham bone to the stockpot. Stir in 2 tablespoons cumin, 2 tablespoons parsley, oregano, salt, black pepper, cayenne and bay leaves. Bring to a boil; reduce heat. Simmer for 2½ to 3 hours or until the beans are tender and the liquid has been reduced by ¾, stirring occasionally.

Remove the ham bone to a plate. Cool slightly. Remove the meat left on the bone and shred. Process about 3 cups of the beans in a blender until puréed. Return the bean purée and ham to the stockpot. Stir in ¼ cup parsley, brown sugar, lemon juice and 1 teaspoon cumin.

Simmer for 30 minutes, stirring frequently. Discard the bay leaves. Taste and adjust the seasonings. Ladle into soup bowls. Top each serving with chopped onions and a dollop of sour cream.

SERVES 6 TO 8

Fort Lauderdale has more active waterways (165 miles) than Venice, Italy (120 miles), thus its nickname, "Venice of America."

Broccoli and Cauliflower Soup

2   **medium onions, finely chopped**
¼   **cup (about) butter**
1   **bunch broccoli**
1   **head cauliflower**
3   **or 4 chicken bouillon cubes (about), or 4 or 5 teaspoons granules**
     Salt and pepper to taste
     Sprigs of parsley

Sauté the onions in the butter in a skillet for 30 to 40 minutes or until dark golden brown. The darker the color, the richer the flavor of the soup.

Cut the stems from the broccoli and cauliflower so only 2 to 3 inches remain. Place in a stockpot, leaving whole if possible. Add just enough water to cover. Add enough bouillon cubes to make a light chicken stock. Bring to a boil. Boil gently until tender. Drain, reserving the liquid.

Spoon the sautéed onions into a blender container. Add about ½ cup of the reserved liquid. Process until smooth. Add some of the broccoli, some of the cauliflower and some of the reserved liquid. Process until puréed. Pour into a large soup tureen. Repeat the process with the remaining broccoli, cauliflower and reserved liquid until of the desired consistency. Season with salt and pepper. Ladle into soup bowls. Top each serving with a sprig of parsley.

SERVES 4

Note: *Chop a small portion of the broccoli and cauliflower and add to the purée to give the soup texture if desired. This soup is great just made with broccoli.*

Chicken Brunswick Stew

1   **(2- to 3-pound) chicken, cut up**
     Garlic salt to taste
2   **(16-ounce) cans cream-style corn**
1   **(16-ounce) can tomatoes, drained, chopped**
1   **(16-ounce) can peas, drained**
1   **(10-ounce) bottle catsup**
½   **cup hickory smoke barbecue sauce**
1   **tablespoon liquid smoke**
1   **tablespoon seasoned salt**
1   **teaspoon cayenne**

Sprinkle the chicken on both sides with garlic salt. Combine the chicken with enough water to cover in a stockpot. Simmer until tender. Drain, reserving the liquid. Chop the chicken into bite-size pieces, discarding the skin and bones.

Combine the chicken, corn, tomatoes, peas, catsup, barbecue sauce, liquid smoke, seasoned salt and cayenne in a large saucepan and mix well. Simmer for 1 to 2 hours, stirring occasionally and adding the reserved liquid as needed for the desired consistency.

SERVES 6 TO 8

Crab Corn Chowder

2	medium onions, chopped
1	cup butter
2	medium red bell peppers, chopped
2	medium green bell peppers, chopped
1	cup flour
1	gallon 2% milk
2	pounds fresh or frozen corn kernels
10	small red potatoes, cut into 1-inch cubes
1	tablespoon thyme
	Tabasco sauce to taste
1	teaspoon salt
1	teaspoon pepper
1	to 2 pounds fresh or canned crab meat
$\frac{1}{2}$	cup chopped chives

Sauté the onions in the butter in a saucepan until tender. Add the red peppers and green peppers and mix well. Stir in the flour. Cook until of the consistency of a roux, stirring constantly. Stir in the milk, corn, potatoes, thyme and Tabasco sauce. Season with the salt and pepper.

Simmer until the potatoes are tender, stirring occasionally. Add the crab meat. Simmer just until heated through, stirring occasionally. Ladle into soup bowls. Sprinkle with the chives.

SERVES 10 TO 15

Grandma's German Lentil Soup

16	to 28 ounces dried lentils
2	yellow onions, chopped
4	carrots, sliced
4	ribs celery, sliced
3	tablespoons butter
1	meaty ham bone
1	teaspoon thyme
2	bay leaves
	Salt and pepper to taste

Sort and rinse the lentils. Sauté the onions, carrots and celery in the butter in a stockpot over medium heat until tender. Add the lentils, ham bone, thyme, bay leaves and just enough water to cover.

Simmer, covered, over low heat for $1\frac{1}{2}$ to 2 hours or until the lentils are tender. Remove the ham bone to a plate. Cut any remaining ham from the bone into bite-size pieces. Return the ham to the stockpot. Discard the bay leaves. Season with salt and pepper. Ladle into soup bowls.

SERVES 12 TO 14

Note: *May prepare in advance and store, covered, in the refrigerator until serving time. Reheat just before serving. Freeze for future use if desired.*

Mushroom Bisque

1   **pound mushrooms, sliced**
1   **medium onion, chopped**
4   **cups chicken broth**
7   **tablespoons butter**
6   **tablespoons flour**
3   **cups milk, heated**
1   **cup whipping cream**
1   **teaspoon salt**
    White pepper to taste
    Tabasco sauce to taste
2   **teaspoons sherry (optional)**

Combine the mushrooms, onion and broth in a saucepan. Simmer, covered, for 30 minutes.

Heat the butter in a saucepan until melted. Stir in the flour. Cook until the mixture is light brown and of a roux consistency, stirring constantly. Add the hot milk, whisking until blended.

Cook until thickened, stirring frequently. Stir in the whipping cream. Add to the mushroom mixture and mix well. Stir in the salt, white pepper and Tabasco sauce. Cook just until heated through, stirring frequently. Stir in the sherry just before serving. Ladle into soup bowls.

SERVES 6 TO 8

Pasta Fagioli

8   **ounces ground beef**
1   **large onion, finely chopped**
4   **cloves of garlic, minced**
10   **cups low-sodium chicken broth**
1   **(19-ounce) can cannellini beans**
1   **(19-ounce) can kidney beans**
8   **ounces pasta**
3   **large tomatoes, chopped**
4   **ribs celery, thinly sliced**
2   **carrots, chopped**
¼   **cup chopped fresh parsley**
2   **tablespoons chopped fresh basil**
2   **tablespoons tomato paste**
1   **teaspoon oregano**
1   **teaspoon red pepper flakes**
    Salt and pepper to taste

Brown the ground beef with the onion and garlic in a stockpot, stirring until the ground beef is crumbly; drain. Add the broth, undrained cannellini beans, undrained kidney beans, pasta, tomatoes, celery, carrots, parsley, basil, tomato paste, oregano, red pepper flakes, salt and pepper and mix well.

Bring to a boil; reduce heat. Simmer, covered, for 30 to 40 minutes or until the pasta is tender and the soup is of the desired consistency, stirring occasionally. Ladle into soup bowls.

SERVES 8

Shrimp and Vegetable Soup

1/3　cup vegetable oil

3　tablespoons flour

2　medium onions, finely chopped

1　pound medium shrimp, peeled, deveined

1　large green bell pepper, coarsely chopped

2　tablespoons chopped fresh parsley

　　Salt and black pepper to taste

　　Red pepper to taste

1　(16-ounce) can whole kernel corn

1　(16-ounce) can whole peeled tomatoes

　　Tabasco sauce to taste

1　cup water

Combine the oil and flour in a saucepan and mix well. Cook over low heat for 30 minutes or until golden brown and of the consistency of a roux, stirring constantly; do not hasten this process. Stir in the onions. Cook for 10 to 15 minutes or until tender, stirring constantly. Stir in the shrimp, green pepper, parsley, salt, black pepper and red pepper. Simmer for 5 to 10 minutes, stirring frequently.

Drain the corn, reserving half the liquid. Stir the corn, reserved liquid, undrained tomatoes, Tabasco sauce and water into the shrimp mixture. Simmer for 1 hour or longer, stirring occasionally and adding additional water as needed for the desired consistency. Ladle into soup bowls.

SERVES 6

Note: *For a stew, add 2 cups cooked long grain rice and cook to a thicker consistency.*

Minted Spinach and Sweet Pea Soup

1/4　cup unsalted butter

2　cups finely chopped yellow onions

1　(10-ounce) package frozen chopped spinach, thawed, drained

3　cups chicken stock

1　(10-ounce) package frozen green peas, thawed

2　cups loosely packed mint leaves

1　cup whipping cream

　　Salt and freshly ground pepper to taste

　　Mint leaves to taste

1　teaspoon nutmeg

Heat the butter in a saucepan until melted. Add the onions and mix well. Cook, covered, over low heat for 25 minutes or until tender and slightly colored. Squeeze the excess moisture from the spinach. Add the spinach, stock and peas to the onion mixture and mix well. Bring to a boil; reduce heat. Simmer, partially covered, for 20 minutes or until the peas are tender, stirring occasionally. Add 2 cups mint and mix well.

Simmer for 5 minutes longer, stirring occasionally. Strain the soup, reserving the liquid. Spoon the vegetable mixture and 1 cup of the reserved liquid into a food processor container fitted with a steel blade. Process until puréed. Return the purée to the saucepan. Stir in the whipping cream and about 1 cup of the reserved liquid or enough to make of the desired consistency. Season with salt and pepper.

Simmer just until heated through, stirring occasionally. Ladle into soup bowls. Top each serving with mint leaves to taste and sprinkle with some of the nutmeg. Serve immediately.

MAKES 1 1/2 QUARTS

COOL AND CRISP

SALADS AND DRESSINGS

Sponsored by

VICTORIA LEE ARTEL
SUE FUHR
CATHY SHEEHAN

An-Apple-A-Day Salad

6   **Braeburn apples, cored, sliced**
1   **cup sliced strawberries**
1/2   **cup seedless green grape halves**
1/2   **cup coarsely chopped walnuts**
1/2   **cup plus 1 tablespoon mayonnaise**
6   **tablespoons milk**
2   **tablespoons honey**
1/2   **to 1 teaspoon cinnamon**
    Red leaf lettuce

Cut the apple slices into halves. Combine the apples, strawberries, grapes and walnuts in a bowl and mix gently.

Whisk the mayonnaise, milk, honey and cinnamon in a bowl. Add to the fruit mixture, tossing to coat. Chill, covered, until serving time. Spoon onto a lettuce-lined serving platter.

SERVES 6

Note: *For variety, serve in orange cups or over papaya halves.*

The manatee is the State Marine Animal. Legend has it that the manatees were actually mermaids. They're large, gentle, and cute, but anyone seeing mermaids must have been at sea too long.

Champagne Salad

8   **ounces cream cheese, softened**
3/4   **cup sugar**
1   **(20-ounce) can crushed pineapple, drained**
1   **(12-ounce) package frozen strawberries, thawed**
2   **bananas, chopped**
1   **cup chopped pecans**
10   **ounces whipped topping**

Beat the cream cheese, sugar, pineapple, strawberries and bananas in a mixer bowl until creamy, scraping the bowl occasionally. Fold in the pecans and whipped topping.

Spoon into a mold. Freeze, covered, until set. Let stand at room temperature for 30 minutes before serving.

SERVES 16

OVERLEAF: *Strawberry Brie Salad*

Cranberry Salad

1   **head Boston or Bibb lettuce**
1   **head romaine**
1   **cup crumbled Gorgonzola cheese**
½   **cup sunflower kernels**
½   **cup dried cranberries**
1   **envelope garlic herb salad dressing mix**
    Olive oil
    Balsamic vinegar

Tear the Boston lettuce and romaine into bite-size pieces. Place in a glass salad bowl. Sprinkle with the cheese, sunflower kernels and cranberries.

Prepare the dressing mix using package directions, substituting olive oil for the salad oil and balsamic vinegar for the cider vinegar. Drizzle over the lettuce mixture and toss to mix.

SERVES 6 TO 8

Fruit Salad with Fresh Mango Sauce

2   **nectarines, sliced**
2   **peaches, peeled, sliced**
1   **small mango, peeled, sliced**
2   **plums, sliced**
1   **pear, cored, cut into quarters, sliced**
½   **small melon, seeded, thinly sliced**
    Juice of 1 lemon
¼   **cup raspberries**
¼   **cup blueberries**
    Mango Sauce
    Sprigs of mint

Arrange the nectarines, peaches, mango, plums, pear and melon on a large plate. Drizzle with the lemon juice. Chill, covered, until serving time or for up to 3 hours in advance of serving.

Arrange the chilled sliced fruit on individual salad plates or on a large serving platter. Spoon the raspberries and blueberries around the sides of the plates. Drizzle with some of the Mango Sauce. Top with the mint. Serve with the remaining Mango Sauce on the side.

SERVES 6

Mango Sauce

1   **large mango, chopped**
    Juice of 3 oranges
    Peel of 1 orange
    Sugar to taste

Process the mango in a food processor until smooth. Add the orange juice, orange peel and sugar. Process until smooth. Press through a strainer into a bowl. Chill, covered, in the refrigerator.

Home-in-Fort Lauderdale Citrus Salad

1   small head red leaf lettuce
1   package romaine hearts
1   bunch watercress, trimmed
     Citrus Dressing
     Sections of 4 navel oranges
     Sections of 2 pink grapefruit
3   avocados, chopped
1   small red onion, thinly sliced,
     chopped
¼   cup dried cranberries (optional)
¼   cup almonds, toasted (optional)

Tear the red leaf lettuce and romaine into bite-size pieces. Combine with the watercress in a salad bowl. Add just enough of the Citrus Dressing to coat and toss. Spoon onto individual salad plates or a serving platter.

Cut the orange and grapefruit sections into bite-size pieces. Arrange the oranges, grapefruit and avocados over the lettuce mixture. Top with the red onion. Sprinkle with the cranberries and/or the almonds. Drizzle with the remaining Citrus Dressing.

SERVES 6 TO 8

The Florida Manatee ranges from 8 to 14 feet long and can weigh up to a ton. In 2000 the manatee population continued its decline to approximately 2,222 individuals.

Citrus Dressing

2   tablespoons fresh orange juice
2   tablespoons fresh lemon juice
1   teaspoon Dijon mustard
½   cup virgin olive oil
2   teaspoons chopped fresh rosemary
     Salt and freshly ground pepper to taste

Combine the orange juice, lemon juice and Dijon mustard in a bowl and mix well. Whisk in the olive oil and rosemary. Season with salt and pepper. Let stand, covered, at room temperature until serving time.

Note: *May be prepared 1 day in advance and stored, covered, in the refrigerator. Bring to room temperature before serving. Add 2 teaspoons honey to the dressing for a slightly sweeter flavor.*

Mandarin Salad

¼ **cup sliced almonds**

1 **tablespoon plus 1 teaspoon sugar**

¼ **head lettuce, torn**

¼ **head romaine, torn**

5 **ribs celery, sliced**

1 **bunch green onions, sliced**
 Sweet-and-Sour Dressing

1 **(11-ounce) can mandarin oranges, drained**

Cook the almonds and sugar in a saucepan over low heat until the almonds are coated, stirring constantly. Spread on an ungreased baking sheet. Let stand until cool. Break into small pieces.

Combine the lettuce, romaine, celery and green onions in a salad bowl. Add the Sweet-and-Sour Dressing, tossing to coat. Mix in the oranges and almonds.

SERVES 8 TO 12

¼ **cup vegetable oil**

2 **tablespoons sugar**

2 **tablespoons vinegar**

1 **tablespoon snipped fresh parsley**

¼ **teaspoon salt**

⅛ **teaspoon pepper**
 Tabasco sauce to taste

Sweet-and-Sour Dressing

Combine the oil, sugar, vinegar, parsley, salt, pepper and Tabasco sauce in a jar with a tightfitting lid. Cover the jar and shake to mix.

Scarlet Fever Salad

1 **pound ground fresh cranberries**

1 **pound Tokay grapes, cut into halves, seeded**

2 **cups sugar**

22 **large marshmallows, chopped**

1 **cup finely chopped pecans**

1 **cup whipping cream**

Combine the cranberries, grapes and sugar in a bowl and mix well. Stir in the marshmallows and pecans.

Beat the whipping cream in a mixer bowl until stiff peaks form. Fold into the cranberry mixture. Chill, covered, for 8 to 10 hours. Stir before serving.

SERVES 8 TO 10

Harvest Pear and Bleu Cheese Salad

Romaine lettuce leaves, torn
3   red pears, cored, thinly sliced
3   green pears, cored, thinly sliced
½   to 1 cup crumbled bleu cheese
½   cup chopped pecans or walnuts (optional)
    Cider Vinaigrette

Layer the romaine, pears, bleu cheese, pecans and Cider Vinaigrette ½ at a time on individual salad plates or a serving platter.

SERVES 15

½   cup vegetable oil or light olive oil
2   tablespoons cider vinegar
1   teaspoon Dijon mustard
¼   teaspoon salt
¼   teaspoon pepper

Cider Vinaigrette

Combine the oil, vinegar, Dijon mustard, salt and pepper in a jar with a tightfitting lid. Cover the jar and shake to mix.

Florida Strawberry and Cucumber Salad

2   tablespoons chopped fresh parsley
1   tablespoon chopped fresh mint
2   teaspoons confectioners' sugar
2½ tablespoons raspberry vinegar
5   tablespoons olive oil
½   English cucumber, thinly sliced
8   ounces Florida strawberries, sliced
    Coarse ground pepper to taste
    Sprigs of mint

Mix the parsley, chopped mint and confectioners' sugar in a bowl. Stir the mixture against the side of the bowl with a wooden spoon to draw out the oils. Stir in the raspberry vinegar and olive oil. Add the cucumber, tossing gently to coat. Marinate, covered, in the refrigerator for up to 2 hours.

Drain the cucumber, reserving the marinade. Arrange the cucumber and strawberries on individual salad plates. Drizzle with the reserved marinade. Sprinkle with pepper. Top with sprigs of mint.

SERVES 4

Strawberry Brie Salad

1½ **cups sliced almonds**
¾ **cup sugar**
2 **heads romaine, torn**
1 **(8-ounce) round Brie cheese, cut into ½-inch pieces**
2 **pints strawberries, sliced**
   Poppy Seed Dressing

Combine the almonds and sugar in a saucepan. Cook over medium heat for 10 minutes or until the sugar begins to melt and the almonds turn light brown, stirring constantly. Cook for 2 to 3 minutes longer, stirring constantly. Spread on a sheet of foil. Let stand until cool. Break into bite-size pieces.

Mix the romaine, cheese, strawberries and almonds in a salad bowl. Drizzle with the Poppy Seed Dressing and toss to coat.

SERVES 8

Note: *May prepare the almonds 1 day in advance. Store in an airtight container.*

Poppy Seed Dressing

½ **cup salad oil**
½ **cup sugar**
⅓ **cup apple cider vinegar**
1½ **teaspoons poppy seeds**
1 **teaspoon dry mustard**
¼ **teaspoon minced onion**

Combine the salad oil, sugar, cider vinegar, poppy seeds, dry mustard and onion in a jar with a tightfitting lid. Cover the jar and shake to mix.

Note: *May be prepared 1 day in advance and stored, covered, in the refrigerator.*

Photograph for this recipe appears on page 44.

Jimmy Buffet, singer, songwriter, and lover of Florida, chaired the Save The Manatee Club in 1981. Under his leadership, the organization drew more than 30,000 members and developed the Adopt-A-Manatee program under the direction of the Florida Audubon Society.

Sweet-and-Sour Chicken Salad

6   boneless skinless chicken breast halves, poached, chopped

1   (8-ounce) can water chestnuts, drained, chopped

1/2   cup chopped celery

1/4   cup chopped pecans

1   small onion, chopped (optional)

1/2   cup mayonnaise

1/2   cup sweet-and-sour sauce

Salt and pepper to taste

Lettuce leaves

Combine the chicken, water chestnuts, celery, pecans and onion in a bowl and mix well. Stir in a mixture of the mayonnaise and sweet-and-sour sauce. Season with salt and pepper.

Spoon onto a lettuce-lined serving platter.

SERVES 4

Note: *Serve on rolls or sandwich bread with a fruit salad on the side for a great lunch menu or a light dinner.*

Chris Evert's Favorite Chicken Salad

4   cups chopped cooked chicken

1   cup pineapple chunks

1   cup celery

1/2   cup chopped scallions

1/4   cup dry-roasted unsalted peanuts

2/3   cup mayonnaise

2   tablespoons chutney

2   tablespoons lemon juice

1/2   teaspoon curry powder

1/2   teaspoon salt

Grated peel of 1/2 lemon

Combine the chicken, pineapple, celery, scallions and peanuts in a bowl and mix well. Stir in a mixture of the mayonnaise, chutney, lemon juice, curry powder, salt and lemon peel. Store, covered, in the refrigerator until serving time.

SERVES 4

Note: *Use fresh pineapple and reduced-fat mayonnaise if desired.*

Chicken and Broccoli Salad

10   to 12 large boneless skinless chicken breast halves

1   onion, cut into quarters

3   bunches broccoli, stalks removed

1   can pitted black olives, drained, cut into 1/4-inch slices

1   package sliced almonds

1   (2-ounce) jar whole pimento, cut into 1/4-inch strips
   Creamy Dressing

Combine the chicken and onion with enough water to cover in a large saucepan. Cook for 25 minutes or until the chicken is tender. Drain, discarding the onion. Let stand until cool. Cut the chicken into 1x2½-inch pieces.

Steam the broccoli in a steamer for 3 minutes. Rinse with cold water to stop the cooking process. Cut the florets into 2-inch pieces.

Reserve some of the broccoli, olives and almonds for the garnish. Mix the chicken, remaining broccoli, pimento, remaining olives, remaining almonds and Creamy Dressing in a bowl. Chill, covered, for 3 hours or longer before serving. Garnish with the reserved broccoli, olives and almonds.

SERVES 20 TO 25

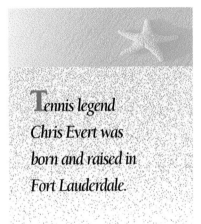

Tennis legend Chris Evert was born and raised in Fort Lauderdale.

Creamy Dressing

1   (32-ounce) jar mayonnaise

5   ribs celery, thinly sliced

1/2   medium red onion, chopped

4   scallions with tops, thinly sliced

1   medium red bell pepper, chopped

1   tablespoon minced garlic

1½   teaspoons curry powder

1½   teaspoons sage

1/2   teaspoon dillweed

1/2   teaspoon thyme

1/8   teaspoon nutmeg
   Salt and freshly ground pepper to taste

Combine the mayonnaise, celery, red onion, scallions, red pepper, garlic, curry powder, sage, dillweed, thyme, nutmeg, salt and pepper in a bowl and mix well. Chill, covered, for 8 to 10 hours before serving.

Curried Chicken and Rice Salad

1   **cup flaked coconut**

2   **teaspoons vegetable oil**

1   **medium onion, finely chopped**

2   **teaspoons curry power**

1/2   **teaspoon ginger**

1   **cup long grain white rice**

2   **cups water**

1/2   **teaspoon salt**

1   **tablespoon plus 1 teaspoon vegetable oil**

1 1/2   **pounds boneless skinless chicken breast halves, chopped**

1   **tablespoon minced garlic**

1   **teaspoon curry powder**

2   **medium ribs celery, finely chopped**

1   **medium red bell pepper, cut into 1/8x1-inch strips**

1/2   **cup currants**

1   **medium Granny Smith apple, cut into 1/4-inch pieces**

    Honey Mustard Vinaigrette (page 65)

3/4   **cup coarsely chopped unsalted dry-roasted peanuts**

3   **medium scallions, coarsely chopped**

    Mixed greens

Spread the coconut on a baking sheet. Toast at 350 degrees for 3 minutes or until golden brown, stirring once or twice. Let stand until cool.

Heat 2 teaspoons oil in a medium saucepan. Add half the onion and mix well. Cook over medium heat for 5 minutes or until tender, stirring constantly. Stir in 2 teaspoons curry powder and the ginger. Cook for 2 minutes, stirring constantly. Mix in the rice, water and salt. Bring to a boil over medium-high heat; reduce heat. Cook, covered, over low heat for 15 minutes or until the rice is tender. Spoon into a bowl.

Heat 1 tablespoon plus 1 teaspoon oil in a skillet over medium heat until hot. Add the chicken. Cook for 5 minutes, stirring occasionally. Add the garlic, remaining onion and 1 teaspoon curry powder. Cook for 2 minutes or until the chicken is tender and cooked through, stirring constantly. Add to the rice and mix well. Let stand until cool.

Stir the celery, red pepper, currants and apple into the rice mixture. Add the Honey Mustard Vinaigrette and toss to coat. Stir in the coconut, peanuts and scallions. Spoon onto a platter lined with mixed greens.

SERVES 6 TO 8

Tropical Sesame Thai Chicken

1   **large Vidalia or red onion, cut into quarters, thinly sliced**

$1/4$ **cup grated gingerroot**

4   **cloves of garlic, minced**

$1/4$ **teaspoon salt**

$1/4$ **teaspoon pepper**

4   **boneless skinless chicken breast halves, cooked, chopped**

1   **(16-ounce) can pineapple chunks, drained (optional)**

1   **red bell pepper, chopped**

1   **yellow bell pepper, chopped**

1   **large carrot, cut lengthwise into halves, thinly sliced**

1   **seedless English cucumber, cut lengthwise into halves,chopped**

1   **(6-ounce) can sliced water chestnuts, drained**

1   **cup cashews, toasted**

$1/4$ **cup sesame seeds, toasted**

      Orange Sesame Dressing

Cook the onion, gingerroot, garlic, salt and pepper in a large skillet sprayed with nonstick cooking spray over medium-low heat for 7 to 8 minutes or until the onion is tender, stirring frequently.

Combine the onion mixture, chicken, pineapple, bell peppers, carrot, cucumber, water chestnuts, cashews and sesame seeds in a salad bowl and mix well. Add the Orange Sesame Dressing and toss to coat. Chill, covered, until serving time.

SERVES 6

$1/2$ **cup chopped fresh parsley or cilantro**

$1/4$ **cup sesame oil**

$1/4$ **cup rice or balsamic vinegar**

$1/4$ **cup soy or tamari sauce**

      Grated zest and juice of 1 orange

3   **tablespoons frozen orange juice concentrate**

2   **tablespoons honey**

2   **teaspoons Asian garlic and chili paste**

Orange Sesame Dressing

Process the parsley, sesame oil, rice vinegar, soy sauce, orange zest, orange juice, orange juice concentrate, honey and garlic and chili paste in a food processor or whisk in a bowl until blended.

Greek Garden Pasta Salad

4	cups drained cooked radiatore
2	cups thinly sliced cucumbers
1/2	small red onion, sliced
1/4	cup kalamata olive halves
1/4	cup finely chopped fresh parsley
1/4	cup olive oil
1/4	cup fresh lemon juice
1/4	cup red wine vinegar
2	teaspoons chopped fresh oregano, or 1/2 teaspoon dried oregano
1/4	teaspoon salt
	Pepper to taste
1/2	cup crumbled feta cheese

Combine the pasta, cucumbers, onion, olives and parsley in a glass bowl and mix gently.

Whisk the olive oil, lemon juice, wine vinegar, oregano, salt and pepper in a bowl. Pour over the pasta mixture, tossing to coat.

Chill, covered, for 1 hour or longer to allow the flavors to marry. Sprinkle with the cheese just before serving.

SERVES 4

Florida ranks first among the states in the production of oranges, grapefruits, tomatoes, watermelons, sugarcane, snap beans, sweet corn, cucumbers, eggplant, green peppers, and radishes.

Italian Salad

16	ounces linguini, penne or small macaroni
2	large bunches scallions, finely chopped
5	or 6 plum tomatoes, chopped
	Pepper to taste
	Garlic salt to taste
1	bottle Italian salad dressing
	Crumbled Gorgonzola cheese to taste

Cook the pasta using package directions until al dente; drain. Combine the pasta, scallions, tomatoes, pepper and garlic salt in a bowl and mix gently. Add the desired amount of salad dressing, tossing to coat. Add the cheese and mix well.

SERVES 6 TO 8

Ham and Bleu Cheese Pasta Salad

8	ounces bow tie pasta or fusilli
4	ounces cooked ham
1	cup pecan pieces
¾	cup crumbled bleu cheese
⅓	cup chopped fresh parsley
⅓	cup olive oil or salad oil
2	tablespoons chopped fresh rosemary
½	teaspoon coarsely ground pepper
1	clove of garlic, minced
	Parmesan cheese to taste

Cook the pasta using package directions; drain. Cut the ham into thin strips. Combine the pasta, ham, pecans, bleu cheese and parsley in a bowl and mix gently. Add a mixture of the olive oil, rosemary, pepper and garlic. Sprinkle with Parmesan cheese and toss. Chill, covered, for several hours before serving.

SERVES 4

Cold Shrimp Pasta Salad

4½	cups water
1½	pounds medium shrimp
16	ounces bow tie pasta or fusilli
1	(6-ounce) package frozen snow peas, thawed, drained
4	medium tomatoes, peeled, chopped, drained
½	red bell pepper, chopped
¼	cup chopped fresh parsley
6	green onions, chopped
¾	cup olive oil
⅓	cup wine vinegar
1½	teaspoons whole basil
1	teaspoon whole oregano
½	teaspoon garlic salt
½	teaspoon coarsely ground pepper
	Shaved Parmesan cheese

Bring the water to a boil in a stockpot. Add the shrimp. Boil for 3 to 5 minutes or until the shrimp turn pink; drain. Rinse with cold water. Chill, covered, in the refrigerator. Peel and devein the shrimp.

Cook the pasta using package directions and omitting the salt; drain. Rinse with cold water and drain. Combine the shrimp, pasta, snow peas, tomatoes, red pepper, parsley and green onions in a bowl and mix gently.

Whisk the olive oil, wine vinegar, basil, oregano, garlic salt and ground pepper in a bowl. Add to the pasta mixture and toss to coat. Chill, covered, for 2 hours or longer. Sprinkle with the cheese just before serving.

SERVES 10

Wild Rice Salad

2   **cups wild rice**

4   **cups water**

¹/₈   **teaspoon salt**

2   **bunches scallion bulbs with 1 inch of tops, thinly sliced**

1   **cup chopped pecans or slivered almonds, toasted**

2   **cups seedless red grapes**

3   **Granny Smith apples, chopped**

³/₄   **cup dried cranberries, currants or raisins**

³/₄   **cup chopped dried apricots**
      Raspberry Dressing

Soak the wild rice in enough cold water to cover in a bowl for 10 minutes; drain. Combine the wild rice, 4 cups water and salt in a saucepan. Bring to a boil; reduce heat. Simmer, covered, for 50 to 60 minutes or until the grains burst open; drain. Let stand until cool.

Combine the wild rice, scallions, pecans, grapes, apples, cranberries and apricots in a bowl and mix well. Add the Raspberry Dressing and toss to coat. Chill, covered, until serving time. You may store, covered, in the refrigerator for several days.

SERVES 8 TO 10

Raspberry Dressing

1   **cup fat-free raspberry vinaigrette**

2   **tablespoons frozen orange juice concentrate**

2   **tablespoons honey**

2   **tablespoons balsamic vinegar**

1   **tablespoon grainy Dijon mustard**

¹/₂   **teaspoon salt**

¹/₄   **teaspoon pepper**

Combine the raspberry vinaigrette, orange juice concentrate, honey, balsamic vinegar, Dijon mustard, salt and pepper in a jar with a tightfitting lid. Cover the jar and shake to mix.

Note: *May substitute a mixture of ³/₄ cup light olive oil and ¹/₄ cup raspberry vinegar for the raspberry vinaigrette.*

Black Bean and Corn Salad with Goat Cheese

1 (16-ounce) can black beans, drained

1 (16-ounce) can whole kernel corn, drained

1 (16-ounce) can lima beans, drained

½ red bell pepper, chopped

4 or 5 green onions with tops, sliced
   Mustard Vinaigrette

3 ounces goat cheese, sliced
   Bread crumbs

Mix the black beans, corn, lima beans, red pepper and green onions in a bowl. Reserve ¼ to ⅓ cup of the Mustard Vinaigrette. Add the remaining Mustard Vinaigrette to the vegetable mixture and toss to coat. Spoon onto individual salad plates.

Dip the cheese in the reserved Mustard Vinaigrette and coat with bread crumbs. Arrange on a baking sheet. Bake at 400 degrees for 10 minutes. Top each serving with the warm goat cheese.

SERVES 4 TO 6

The Hillsboro Inlet Lighthouse was built in 1906 to warn seafarers of the dangerous northern tip of the Florida Reef. Measuring 136 feet tall, the lighthouse is on the National Register and is still a working lighthouse.

Mustard Vinaigrette

5 tablespoons extra-virgin olive oil

1 tablespoon Dijon mustard

1 tablespoon red wine vinegar
   Herbs to taste

Combine the olive oil, Dijon mustard, wine vinegar and herbs in a jar with a tightfitting lid. Cover the jar and shake to mix.

Four-Cheese Salad

1   pound bacon, crisp-fried, crumbled
1   head iceberg lettuce, torn
1   head romaine, torn
1   red bell pepper, chopped
6   green onions, sliced
1   cup freshly shredded mozzarella cheese
¾   cup freshly grated Romano cheese
½   cup each freshly grated Parmesan and provolone cheese
    Croutons
    Italian Vinaigrette

Toss the bacon, iceberg lettuce, romaine, red pepper, green onions, mozzarella cheese, Romano cheese, Parmesan cheese and provolone cheese in a bowl. Add the Croutons and Italian Vinaigrette just before serving. Toss to mix.

SERVES 12 TO 15

Note: *Using freshly grated or shredded cheeses is a must for this recipe. Grate or shred in different sizes to give a contrast in texture.*

6   English muffins, cubed
½   cup Italian Vinaigrette
¼   cup grated Parmesan cheese

Croutons

Toss the muffin cubes with the Italian Vinaigrette and cheese. Arrange in a single layer on a baking sheet. Bake at 350 degrees for 30 minutes or until golden brown, stirring every 5 to 10 minutes. Let stand until cool. May be prepared in advance and stored in a sealable plastic bag.

1¼ cups sugar
1   cup white wine vinegar
6   anchovies or equivalent amount of anchovy paste
½   cup dried oregano
¼   cup cornstarch
2   teaspoons pepper
1½ teaspoons garlic salt
1   teaspoon salt
¾   cup olive oil
¾   cup vegetable oil

Italian Vinaigrette

Process the sugar, wine vinegar, anchovies, oregano, cornstarch, pepper, garlic salt and salt in a blender until smooth. Add the olive oil and vegetable oil gradually, processing constantly until combined. Store, covered, in the refrigerator. Use ½ cup to prepare the croutons, and drizzle the remainder over the salad.

Lively Corn Salad

1   (48-ounce) package frozen white corn

3   (11-ounce) cans yellow niblet corn, drained

1   (28-ounce) can diced tomatoes, drained

2   green bell peppers, chopped

2   purple onions, chopped

2   large cucumbers, peeled, chopped

1   cup sour cream

1/2   cup mayonnaise

1/4   cup white vinegar

4   teaspoons salt

1   teaspoon celery seeds

1   teaspoon dry mustard

1   teaspoon pepper

4   ripe tomatoes, chopped

Mix the white corn, yellow corn, canned tomatoes, green peppers, onions and cucumbers in a bowl.

Combine the sour cream, mayonnaise, vinegar, salt, celery seeds, dry mustard and pepper in a bowl and mix well. Add to the vegetable mixture and toss to coat. Chill, covered, for 24 hours or longer. Drain and stir in the fresh tomatoes just before serving.

SERVES 25

Tangy Cucumber Salad

1 1/2   cups sugar

1   cup white vinegar

1   tablespoon celery seeds

1   tablespoon mustard seeds

1 1/2   teaspoons turmeric

3   or 4 large cucumbers, peeled, sliced

1   large onion, thinly sliced

Combine the sugar, vinegar, celery seeds, mustard seeds and turmeric in a bowl and mix well. Add the cucumbers and onion and mix gently. Marinate, covered, in the refrigerator.

SERVES 6 TO 8

Note: *As the vegetables disappear, add additional cucumbers and onions to the marinade. The marinade may be stored in the refrigerator for up to 1 week.*

Belgian Endive Salad

6   **ounces herbed cheese spread**

1   **to 2 heads Belgian endive, separated into spears**

6   **ounces Gorgonzola cheese, crumbled**

½   **cup finely chopped sun-dried tomatoes**

     Balsamic vinegar to taste

Spoon ½ teaspoon of the cheese spread onto the stem end of each endive spear. Sprinkle with the Gorgonzola cheese and sun-dried tomatoes. Arrange the endive spears on 4 salad plates. Drizzle with the balsamic vinegar.

SERVES 4

Ginger Sesame Salad

4   **heads Boston or Bibb lettuce, torn**

2   **cups shredded cooked chicken**

     Sesame seeds to taste

     Sesame Dressing

Toss the lettuce, chicken and sesame seeds in a salad bowl. Add the Sesame Dressing and mix well.

SERVES 6 TO 8

Sesame Dressing

3   **tablespoons seasoned rice vinegar**

1   **tablespoon soy sauce**

1   **tablespoon ground arrowroot**

2   **tablespoons honey**

⅓   **cup defatted chicken broth**

¼   **cup pineapple juice**

2   **teaspoons oriental sesame oil**

1   **teaspoon grated gingerroot**

1   **clove of garlic, minced**

Whisk the vinegar, soy sauce and arrowroot in a saucepan until mixed. Add the honey, stirring until blended. Stir in the broth, pineapple juice, sesame oil, gingerroot and garlic.

     Cook over medium heat until thickened, stirring constantly. Remove from heat. Let stand until cool. Chill, covered, until serving time.

Gourmet Club Salad

¾ **cup extra-virgin olive oil**

1 **small onion, grated**

¼ **cup tarragon vinegar**

3 **tablespoons sugar**

2 **tablespoons lemon juice**

2 **tablespoons catsup, or to taste**

1 **teaspoon garlic salt**

¼ **teaspoon dry mustard or
   1 teaspoon Chinese mustard**

¼ **teaspoon Tabasco sauce
   Roquefort cheese, crumbled**

1 **head romaine lettuce, torn**

Combine the olive oil, onion, tarragon vinegar, sugar, lemon juice, catsup, garlic salt, dry mustard and Tabasco sauce in a jar with a tightfitting lid. Cover the jar and shake to mix. Add the cheese and shake gently. Pour the desired amount of the dressing over the lettuce in a salad bowl and toss to coat.

SERVES 6 TO 8

Mixed Field Greens with Bleu Cheese and Capers

¼ **cup pine nuts**

1 **package mesclun**

4 **ounces bleu cheese, crumbled**

2 **ounces capers, drained**

¼ **cup raisins**

½ **cup balsamic vinegar**

½ **cup olive oil
   Freshly ground pepper to taste
   Garlic salt to taste**

Spread the pine nuts evenly on a baking sheet. Broil for 1 to 2 minutes or until toasted. Toss the pine nuts, mesclun, cheese, capers and raisins in a salad bowl. Chill, covered, until serving time.

Whisk the balsamic vinegar and olive oil in a bowl. Season with pepper and garlic salt. Drizzle over the mesclun mixture just before serving.

SERVES 4

Lemon Tarragon Chicken Salad

1   **seedless English cucumber, cut lengthwise into halves**

1   **bunch scallion bulbs with 1-inch tops, thinly sliced**

4   **boneless skinless chicken breast halves, cooked, cut into $1/2$-inch pieces**

2   **cups seedless red grapes**

1   **cup chopped honeydew or cantaloupe**

1   **cup pecan halves or slivered almonds, toasted**

      Creamy Lemon Tarragon Dressing

Slice the cucumber halves lengthwise and thinly slice. Combine the cucumber, scallions, chicken, grapes, melon and pecans in a salad bowl and toss gently. Add the Creamy Lemon Tarragon Dressing and toss to coat. Chill, covered, until serving time.

SERVES 6

Fort Lauderdale was named for Major William Lauderdale, a Tennessee volunteer who came down with his troops and built a fort to protect the white residents from the Indians.

Creamy Lemon Tarragon Dressing

2   **cups fat-free or light mayonnaise**

$1/2$ **cup chopped fresh parsley**

      Grated zest and juice of 2 lemons

3   **tablespoons finely chopped fresh tarragon leaves**

1   **tablespoon tarragon vinegar**

1   **tablespoon grainy Dijon mustard**

$1/2$ **teaspoon salt**

$1/4$ **teaspoon pepper**

Process the mayonnaise, parsley, lemon zest, lemon juice, tarragon, tarragon vinegar, Dijon mustard, salt and pepper in a food processor or mix in a large bowl until blended.

Marinated Vegetable Salad

1	**pound mushrooms**
2	**small zucchini, sliced**
	Florets of 1 bunch broccoli
2	**carrots, sliced**
2	**red onions, sliced, separated into rings**
3	**ribs celery, sliced**
	Florets of 1 head cauliflower
1	**red bell pepper, julienned**
1	**green bell pepper, julienned**
1	**cup salad oil**
½	**cup cider vinegar**
2	**cloves of garlic, minced**
3	**tablespoons sugar**
2	**teaspoons salt**
½	**teaspoon pepper**
1	**(4-ounce) can pitted black olives, drained (optional)**

Mix the mushrooms, zucchini, broccoli, carrots, onions, celery, cauliflower, red pepper and green pepper in a bowl. Pour a mixture of the salad oil, vinegar, garlic, sugar, salt and pepper over the vegetables and toss to coat. Marinate, covered, in the refrigerator for 3 days, stirring frequently. Add the black olives just before serving.

SERVES 10

Note: *Choose any combination of the vegetables mentioned or use the entire list in the salad. May double or triple the marinade, depending on the amount of vegetables used.*

Honey Mustard Vinaigrette

¼	**cup red wine vinegar**
1	**tablespoon fresh lemon juice**
1	**tablespoon honey**
1	**tablespoon Dijon mustard**
1	**teaspoon minced garlic**
¼	**cup plus 2 tablespoons vegetable oil**
2	**teaspoons salt**
¾	**teaspoon freshly ground pepper**

Whisk the wine vinegar, lemon juice, honey, Dijon mustard and garlic in a bowl. Add the oil, whisking constantly until mixed. Stir in the salt and pepper.

MAKES ¾ CUP

RISE AND SHINE

BRUNCH AND BREADS

Sponsored by
BOARD OF DIRECTORS
1997–1999

Sunny Day Apple Butter

4   pounds Braeburn apples, peeled, cored, coarsely chopped
½   cup apple juice
½   cup Florida orange juice
¼   cup fresh lemon juice
½   cup sugar
⅓   cup packed brown sugar
1   teaspoon cinnamon
¼   teaspoon nutmeg
1   (½x4-inch strip) orange peel

Combine the apples, apple juice, orange juice and lemon juice in a saucepan. Bring to a boil; reduce heat. Simmer, covered, for 10 minutes or until the apples are tender, stirring occasionally.

Process half the apple mixture in a food processor until puréed. May mash with a hand masher. Combine the purée with the remaining apple mixture and mix well. Stir in the sugar, brown sugar, cinnamon, nutmeg and orange peel. Spoon into an 8x8-inch baking dish.

Bake at 350 degrees for 1 hour or until thickened and dark in color, stirring frequently. Discard peel. Let stand until cool. Spoon into a covered bowl or jar with a tightfitting lid. Store in the refrigerator.

MAKES 3 CUPS

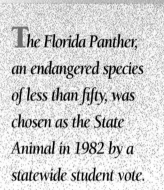

The Florida Panther, an endangered species of less than fifty, was chosen as the State Animal in 1982 by a statewide student vote.

Apple Dip

8   ounces cream cheese, softened
¾   cup packed brown sugar
¼   cup confectioners' sugar
1   tablespoon milk
½   teaspoon vanilla extract
6   to 8 Granny Smith apples, cut into wedges

Beat the cream cheese, brown sugar, confectioners' sugar, milk and vanilla in a mixer bowl until smooth and creamy, scraping the bowl occasionally. Serve at room temperature with the apples.

SERVES 6 TO 8

OVERLEAF: *Lin's Tropical Banana Bread*

Old-Fashioned Granola

2½ cups rolled oats

1 cup shredded coconut

½ cup chopped walnuts or almonds

½ cup sesame seeds

½ cup sunflower kernels

½ cup unsweetened wheat germ

½ cup honey

¼ cup vegetable oil

½ cup chopped dried apricots

½ cup raisins

Combine the oats, coconut, walnuts, sesame seeds, sunflower kernels and wheat germ in a bowl and mix well. Stir in a mixture of the honey and oil. Spread in a 9x13-inch baking pan.

Bake at 300 degrees for 45 to 50 minutes or until light brown, stirring every 15 minutes. Remove from oven. Stir in the apricots and raisins. Spread on a baking sheet to cool, stirring occasionally to prevent lumps from forming. Store in an airtight container.

MAKES 6½ CUPS

Note: *This is great not only as a cereal but also delicious sprinkled over vanilla ice cream.*

Day-Ahead Egg Casserole

24 eggs

½ cup milk

¼ to ⅓ cup (about) butter

2 (10-ounce) cans cream of mushroom soup

2 (3-ounce) cans mushrooms, drained

½ cup sherry

1 green bell pepper, minced

2 cups shredded sharp Cheddar cheese

Whisk the eggs and milk in a bowl until blended. Scramble the eggs in the butter in a skillet until of the desired degree of doneness; drain. Spread in a buttered baking pan.

Mix the soup, mushrooms, sherry and green pepper in a bowl. Spread over the eggs. Sprinkle with the cheese. Chill, covered, for 8 to 10 hours. Bake at 325 degrees for 50 minutes.

SERVES 15

Cheesy Egg English Muffins

12	hard-cooked eggs, chopped
1	pound sharp Cheddar cheese, shredded
1/4	cup grated Parmesan cheese, or to taste
1	small to medium onion, finely chopped
8	ounces bacon, crisp-fried, crumbled
1	tablespoon spicy mustard
2	teaspoons Worcestershire sauce or soy sauce, or to taste
1/2	teaspoon Tabasco sauce, or to taste
1/2	teaspoon freshly ground pepper, or to taste
1/2	teaspoon garlic powder, or to taste
3/4	cup (about) mayonnaise
8	English muffins, split

Combine the eggs, Cheddar cheese, Parmesan cheese, onion, bacon, mustard, Worcestershire sauce, Tabasco sauce, pepper and garlic powder in a bowl and mix well. Add just enough mayonnaise to bind the ingredients and mix well.

Spread the egg mixture over the cut sides of the muffins. Arrange on a baking sheet. Broil until bubbly. Serve immediately.

SERVES 8

Note: *Great make-ahead breakfast for when you have house guests.*

Apple and Cheddar Quiche

1	large cooking apple, shredded
1/2	cup white port or sauterne
1	all ready pie pastry
1 1/2	cups shredded Cheddar cheese
1 1/2	cups whipping cream or half-and-half
3	eggs
1/4	teaspoon nutmeg
	Apple slices
	Shredded Cheddar cheese

Combine the shredded apple and wine in a bowl and mix well. Marinate for 1 hour or longer; drain. Fit the pastry into a 10-inch quiche pan.

Sprinkle the marinated apple and 1 1/2 cups cheese over the bottom of the prepared quiche pan. Beat the whipping cream, eggs and nutmeg in a mixer bowl until blended. Pour into the prepared pan.

Bake at 375 degrees for 40 to 50 minutes or until a knife inserted 1 inch from the edge comes out clean. Let stand for 15 minutes before serving. Arrange apple slices in a decorative pattern over the top. Sprinkle with Cheddar cheese.

SERVES 4 TO 6

Caramel Crescent Rolls

5 tablespoons butter

¾ cup packed brown sugar

¼ cup water

2 (8-count) cans crescent rolls

3 tablespoons butter, softened

¼ cup cinnamon

¼ cup sugar

Place 5 tablespoons butter in a 9x13-inch baking pan. Heat at 375 degrees until melted. Remove the pan from the oven. Add the brown sugar and water, stirring until the brown sugar dissolves and tilting the pan to cover the bottom evenly.

Unroll the crescent roll dough. Separate each can into 4 rectangles and press the perforations to seal. Spread 3 tablespoons butter on the rectangles. Sprinkle generously with a mixture of the cinnamon and sugar.

Roll each rectangle starting at the short end to form a log. Cut each log into 4 equal slices. Place cut side down in the prepared baking pan. Bake at 375 degrees for 20 to 25 minutes or until golden brown. Invert immediately onto a serving platter. Serve warm with milk.

MAKES 32 ROLLS

Nationally known novelist John D. MacDonald introduced a series of books based in the Fort Lauderdale area, including Flash of Green, The Deep Blue Goodbye and The Empty Copper Sea. His book The Executioners became the twice-filmed movie, Cape Fear.

Apple Pancake

½ cup flour

½ cup milk, at room temperature

3 eggs, at room temperature

2 large Rome Beauty apples, peeled, cored, thinly sliced

2 tablespoons butter or margarine

½ cup sugar

2 tablespoons cinnamon

Process the flour, milk and eggs in a blender until mixed. Sauté the apples in half the butter in a 10- or 12-inch ovenproof skillet until tender. Pour the egg mixture over the apples.

Bake at 500 degrees for 10 minutes or until puffy and brown around the edge. Dot with the remaining butter. Mix the sugar and cinnamon in a bowl. Sprinkle the desired amount over the top. Bake for 5 to 10 minutes longer or until the sugar melts.

SERVES 2

Stuffed French Toast

20   **slices bread, crusts trimmed, cubed**

16   **ounces cream cheese, cubed**
      Cinnamon to taste

12   **eggs, beaten**

1¾ **cups milk**

⅓   **cup maple syrup**

1   **teaspoon vanilla extract**
      Confectioners' sugar

Spread half the bread cubes in a baking pan sprayed with nonstick cooking spray. Arrange the cream cheese over the bread. Sprinkle generously with cinnamon. Top with the remaining bread cubes.

Whisk the eggs, milk, maple syrup and vanilla in a bowl until blended. Pour over the prepared layers. Chill, covered, for 8 to 10 hours.

Bake at 375 degrees for 45 minutes. Sprinkle with confectioners' sugar. Serve with warm syrup.

SERVES 15

Tropical Wheat Berry Breakfast Cereal

1   **cup wheat berries**

3½ **cups water**

1   **cup whole wheat or regular couscous**

1   **cup chopped dried mangoes or apricots**

1   **cup chopped macadamia nuts or pecans, toasted**

½   **cup candied pineapple or dried cranberries**

½   **cup chopped dates or raisins**

½   **cup shredded coconut (optional)**
      Grated zest and juice of 2 oranges

½   **cup honey, heated**

¼   **cup frozen orange juice concentrate**

Combine the wheat berries with enough cold water to cover in a bowl. Soak for 8 to 10 hours; drain. Combine the wheat berries and 2 cups of the water in a saucepan. Bring to a boil; reduce heat to medium-low. Simmer, covered, for 90 minutes or until the wheat berry grains burst open and are tender, adding additional water as needed; drain.

Bring the remaining 1½ cups water to a boil in a saucepan. Pour over the couscous in a heatproof bowl. Let stand, covered, until cool. Fluff the couscous with a fork. Stir in the wheat berries. Add the mangoes, macadamia nuts, pineapple, dates and coconut. Add a mixture of the orange zest, orange juice, honey and orange juice concentrate and mix well. Serve chilled or at room temperature.

SERVES 6 TO 8

Lin's Tropical Banana Bread

1½ **cups sugar**

½ **cup vegetable oil**

¼ **cup dark rum**

2 **ripe bananas, mashed**

2 **eggs**

1 **tablespoon milk**

1 **teaspoon vanilla extract**

1¾ **cups unbleached flour, sifted**

2 **tablespoons dry buttermilk blend**

1 **teaspoon baking soda**

½ **teaspoon salt**

½ **cup finely chopped walnuts**

½ **cup chopped pecans**

¼ **cup finely grated coconut (optional)**

Rum Glaze

Combine the sugar, oil, rum, bananas, eggs, milk and vanilla in a mixer bowl. Beat until blended, scraping the bowl occasionally.

Mix the flour, buttermilk blend, baking soda and salt in a bowl. Add to the banana mixture, mixing just until moistened; do not overmix.

Spoon the batter into a greased 5x9-inch loaf pan. Sprinkle the walnuts, pecans and coconut over the top. Bake at 325 degrees for 45 minutes or until the edges pull from the sides of the pan. Remove the bread from the pan (pecans and coconut should be on top). Drizzle with the warm Rum Glaze. Serve warm or chill for later use.

MAKES 1 LOAF

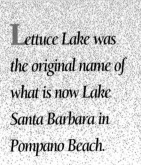

Lettuce Lake was the original name of what is now Lake Santa Barbara in Pompano Beach.

Rum Glaze

¼ **cup sugar**

2 **tablespoons butter**

2 **tablespoons water**

¼ **cup dark rum**

Combine the sugar, butter and water in a microwave-safe bowl. Microwave until boiling. Boil for 1 to 2 minutes. Stir in the rum. May boil in a saucepan for 5 minutes.

Photograph for this recipe appears on page 66.

Bimini Bread

¹/₃ **cup boiling water**
¹/₄ **cup flaked coconut**
1 **cup flour**
¹/₃ **cup sugar**
1 **envelope fast-rising yeast**
6 **tablespoons melted butter**
1 **egg**
1 **cup (about) flour**

Pour the boiling water over the coconut in a bowl. Let stand for 5 minutes. This makes coconut milk. Combine 1 cup flour, sugar and yeast in a bowl.

Strain the coconut milk into the butter in a glass measuring cup. Microwave just until warm to the touch. Stir the butter mixture into the flour mixture with a wooden spoon. Add the egg and mix well. Add 1 cup flour, stirring until the dough is no longer sticky. May add additional flour if needed for the desired consistency.

Knead the dough on a lightly floured surface until smooth and elastic. Let rest, covered, for 10 to 15 minutes. Punch the dough down. Shape into a loaf in a greased 5x9-inch loaf pan. Let rise, covered with a tea towel, until doubled in bulk. Bake at 325 degrees for 40 minutes or until golden brown. Invert onto a wire rack to cool.

MAKES 1 LOAF

Sour Cream Coffee Cake

¹/₂ **cup butter, softened**
1 **cup sugar**
2 **eggs**
1 **teaspoon vanilla extract**
1¹/₂ **cups sour cream**
2 **cups sifted flour**
1 **teaspoon baking soda**
1 **teaspoon baking powder**
¹/₂ **teaspoon salt**
¹/₂ **cup packed brown sugar**
¹/₂ **cup sugar**
1¹/₂ **teaspoons cinnamon**

Beat the butter in a mixer bowl until creamy. Add 1 cup sugar and beat until blended. Add the eggs 1 at a time, beating well after each addition. Mix in the vanilla. Beat in the sour cream. Mix the flour, baking soda, baking powder and salt in a bowl.

Spoon ¹/₄ of the flour mixture into a bowl. Add ¹/₃ of the sour cream mixture and mix well. Continue this combining process until all of the flour mixture and all of the sour cream mixture has been used, beginning and ending with the flour mixture. Spoon ¹/₂ of the mixture into a greased and floured 9x13-inch baking pan.

Combine the brown sugar, ¹/₂ cup sugar and cinnamon in a bowl. Sprinkle half of the brown sugar mixture over the prepared layer. Top with the remaining batter and sprinkle with the remaining brown sugar mixture. Bake at 325 degrees for 35 to 40 minutes or until the edges begin to pull from the sides of the pan.

SERVES 12 TO 15

Cranberry Orange Nut Bread

2   **cups flour**

1   **cup sugar**

1½   **teaspoons baking powder**

1   **teaspoon salt**

½   **teaspoon baking soda**

¼   **cup margarine**

⅔   **cup orange juice**

1   **egg, beaten**

1   **tablespoon grated orange peel**

1   **cup coarsely chopped cranberries**

½   **cup chopped nuts**

Sift the flour, sugar, baking powder, salt and baking soda into a bowl and mix well. Cut in the margarine until crumbly.

Whisk the orange juice, egg and orange peel in a bowl. Add to the flour mixture, stirring just until moistened. Fold in the cranberries and nuts. Spoon into a greased loaf pan. Bake at 350 degrees for 1 hour or until the loaf tests done.

MAKES 1 LOAF

Irish Soda Bread

2   **cups flour**

3   **tablespoons sugar**

1   **tablespoon caraway seeds**

1   **teaspoon baking powder**

½   **teaspoon baking soda**

½   **teaspoon salt**

3   **tablespoons unsalted butter**

⅔   **cup dark raisins**

¾   **cup buttermilk**

1   **tablespoon melted unsalted butter**

1½   **teaspoons sugar**

Mix the flour, 3 tablespoons sugar, caraway seeds, baking powder, baking soda and salt in a bowl. Cut in 3 tablespoons butter until crumbly. Stir in the raisins. Add the buttermilk gradually and mix well.

Knead the dough on a lightly floured surface for 5 minutes or until smooth and elastic. Shape into a ball. Place in a greased round 8-inch baking pan. Cut a cross ⅔ through the center of the dough. Brush the top with 1 tablespoon melted butter and sprinkle with 1½ teaspoons sugar. Bake at 350 degrees for 30 minutes or until the loaf tests done. Remove to a wire rack to cool.

MAKES 1 LOAF

Note: *May substitute a mixture of 1 beaten egg and ¼ cup skim milk for the buttermilk.*

Poppy Seed Almond Bread

3 cups flour

2¼ cups sugar

1½ cups milk

1 cup plus 2 tablespoons vegetable oil

3 eggs

1½ tablespoons poppy seeds

1½ teaspoons salt

1½ teaspoons baking powder

1½ teaspoons vanilla extract

1½ teaspoons almond extract

1½ teaspoons butter flavoring

Orange Glaze

Combine the flour, sugar, milk, oil, eggs, poppy seeds, salt, baking powder and flavorings in a mixer bowl. Beat for 1 to 2 minutes or until mixed, scraping the bowl occasionally. Spoon into 3 greased 4x8-inch loaf pans. Bake at 355 degrees for 55 minutes or until the loaves test done. Cool in pans on wire racks for 15 minutes.

Brush the tops of the warm loaves with the Orange Glaze. Cool for 30 to 45 minutes longer. Remove the loaves from the pans. Serve warm, at room temperature or chill if desired.

MAKES 3 LOAVES

Fort Lauderdale's first woman city commissioner was Genevieve Pynchon, who took office in 1937.

Orange Glaze

¾ cup sifted confectioners' sugar

¼ cup orange juice

1½ teaspoons almond extract

1½ teaspoons vanilla extract

1½ teaspoons butter flavoring

Combine the confectioners' sugar, orange juice and flavorings in a saucepan. Cook over low heat until blended and of a glaze consistency, stirring frequently.

Honey Harvest Muffins

2   cups unbleached flour
1/3   cup sugar
1   tablespoon baking powder
1   teaspoon cinnamon
1/4   teaspoon baking soda
1/4   teaspoon ground allspice
1/4   teaspoon ground nutmeg
1   cup orange juice
1/3   cup vegetable oil
1/4   cup pure maple syrup
1   egg
1   teaspoon vanilla extract
1   large apple
1   cup organic raisins
3/4   cup coarsely chopped walnuts
        Cinnamon and sugar to taste
3   tablespoons honey

Combine the flour, 1/3 cup sugar, baking powder, 1 teaspoon cinnamon, baking soda, allspice and nutmeg in a bowl and mix well. Whisk the orange juice, oil, maple syrup, egg and vanilla in a bowl. Add the flour mixture, stirring just until moistened; do not overmix.

Peel and core the apple. Cut 18 very small pieces from the apple and reserve. Chop the remaining apple. Fold the remaining apple, raisins and walnuts into the batter. Spoon the batter into 6 greased jumbo muffin cups. Top each with 3 pieces of the reserved apple. Sprinkle lightly with cinnamon and sugar to taste.

Bake at 400 degrees for 30 to 35 minutes or until a wooden pick inserted in the center comes out clean. Drizzle 1 1/2 teaspoons of honey over each muffin.

MAKES 6 JUMBO MUFFINS

Oatmeal Scones

1   cup flour
1   tablespoon sugar
1   teaspoon baking soda
1/2   teaspoon salt
1/4   teaspoon cream of tartar
1   cup rolled oats
1/4   cup raisins
1/4   cup butter
3/4   cup buttermilk

Sift the flour, sugar, baking soda, salt and cream of tartar into a bowl and mix well. Stir in the oats and raisins. Cut in the butter until crumbly. Add the buttermilk and mix gently.

Pat the dough into an 8-inch circle on a lightly floured surface. Score the top into 6 wedges. Place on a greased baking sheet. Bake at 400 degrees for 20 minutes.

SERVES 6

EASTSIDE ENTREES

MEATS

POULTRY

SEAFOOD

PASTA

Sponsored by **North Broward Hospital District**

Beef Brisket

2   **tablespoons liquid smoke**

2   **teaspoons celery salt**

2   **teaspoons Worcestershire sauce**

1   **teaspoon each garlic salt and onion salt**

    Pepper to taste

1   **(3- to 4-pound) beef brisket**

1   **cup barbecue sauce**

Combine the liquid smoke, celery salt, Worcestershire sauce, garlic salt, onion salt and pepper in a bowl and mix well. Brush over the entire surface of the brisket. Place in a baking pan.

Bake, covered with foil, at 300 degrees for 4 hours; remove foil. Pour the barbecue sauce over the brisket. Bake for 1 hour longer.

SERVES 6

Fort Lauderdale was incorporated in 1911 but was not officially made a city until June 1917, because it did not have the required 300 registered voters until then.

Spirited Eye-of-Round

1   **(2½-pound) eye-of-round roast**

    Seasoned salt to taste

    Lemon pepper and meat tenderizer to taste

¼   **cup soy sauce**

2   **tablespoons Italian salad dressing**

2   **tablespoons bourbon or whiskey**

2   **tablespoons Worcestershire sauce**

Pierce the roast in several places with a sharp knife. Sprinkle lightly with seasoned salt, lemon pepper and meat tenderizer. Place the roast in a sealable plastic bag and set in a bowl.

Mix the soy sauce, salad dressing, bourbon and Worcestershire sauce in a bowl. Pour over the roast; seal tightly. Marinate in the refrigerator for 8 to 10 hours, turning occasionally. Place the roast in a baking pan.

Roast at 325 degrees for 1¼ to 1¾ hours or until a meat thermometer registers 140 degrees. Let rest for several minutes. Cut into ½-inch slices.

SERVES 8 TO 10

OVERLEAF: *Clockwise from top left: Pork Medallions with Sautéed Apples, Captain Bill's Baby Snapper Fillets, Florida Clambake, Escargot-Stuffed Tenderloin*

Pot Roast with Raisin Sauce

¼   **cup olive oil**

     Juice of 1 lemon

2   **bay leaves, crushed**

1   **medium onion, minced**

2   **teaspoons allspice**

     Salt and pepper to taste

1   **(5-pound) rolled rump roast**

2   **tablespoons butter**

2   **tablespoons flour**

6   **cups (about) boiling water**

     Flour

     Milk

½   **cup raisins**

Whisk the olive oil and lemon juice in a bowl. Stir in the bay leaves, onion, allspice, salt and pepper. Rub the mixture over the roast.

Brown the roast on all sides in the butter in a roasting pan. Stir in 2 tablespoons flour. Add just enough boiling water to reach halfway up the sides of the roast and mix well. Bake, covered, at 350 degrees for 2½ to 3 hours or until of the desired degree of doneness.

Transfer the roast to a serving platter, reserving the pan drippings. Stir equal portions of flour and milk into the reserved drippings and mix well. Cook until thickened, stirring constantly. Spoon the raisins into a gravy boat. Pour the hot gravy over the raisins. Serve with the roast.

SERVES 4

Escargot-Stuffed Tenderloin

1   **(3½-pound) beef tenderloin**

3   **cloves of garlic, minced**

2   **tablespoons butter**

1   **can escargot**

     Salt and pepper to taste

3   **or 4 slices bacon**

Cut a horizontal slit in the top of the tenderloin, leaving the ends and bottom third intact to form a pocket. Sauté the garlic in the butter in a skillet until light brown. Add the escargot and mix well. Sauté for 1½ minutes or until heated through. Season with salt and pepper.

Spoon the escargot mixture into the pocket. Lay the bacon slices crosswise over the tenderloin. Place in a baking pan. Bake at 425 degrees for 15 minutes. Reduce the oven temperature to 350 degrees. Bake for 20 minutes longer or until a meat thermometer registers 130 degrees for rare or 140 degrees for medium.

SERVES 12 TO 15

Photograph for this recipe appears on page 78.

81

Beef Stroganoff

1	(1½-pound) beef fillet
	Salt and pepper to taste
3	tablespoons unsalted butter
1	tablespoon vegetable oil
1	cup chopped onion
2	large cloves of garlic, minced
8	ounces portobello mushrooms, thinly sliced
8	ounces white mushrooms
½	cup dry white wine
½	cup beef broth
2	cups sour cream
2	tablespoons Dijon mustard

Cut the fillet into 1-inch slices. Sprinkle with salt and pepper. Heat 1 tablespoon of the butter and oil in a skillet until hot. Sear the beef in batches in the butter mixture. Remove the beef to a platter with a slotted spoon, reserving the pan drippings.

Heat the remaining 2 tablespoons butter with the reserved pan drippings. Add the onion and garlic. Cook over medium heat until the onion is tender, stirring frequently. Stir in the mushrooms, salt and pepper. Cook over high heat until the liquid evaporates, stirring frequently. Add the wine.

Bring to a boil. Boil for 3 minutes, stirring constantly. Return the beef to the skillet and mix well. Stir in the broth, sour cream and Dijon mustard. Cook just until heated through, stirring frequently; do not boil. Serve over hot cooked pasta or rice.

SERVES 4 TO 6

Tropical Steak and Portobello Kabobs

2	cups pineapple juice
½	cup soy sauce
1	clove of garlic, crushed
1	(2-inch) piece gingerroot, julienned
1	teaspoon honey
1½	to 2 pounds cubed sirloin
1	small onion
1	large red bell pepper
8	ounces portobello mushrooms
	Olive oil to taste
1	pineapple, cut into chunks

Combine the pineapple juice, soy sauce, garlic, gingerroot and honey in a bowl and mix well. Pour over the sirloin cubes in a sealable plastic bag, tossing to coat. Marinate in the refrigerator for 6 to 10 hours, turning occasionally.

Chop the onion, red pepper and mushrooms into 1- to 1½-inch pieces. Drizzle with olive oil.

Thread the sirloin, onion, red pepper, mushrooms and pineapple alternately on skewers until all of the ingredients are used. Grill over hot coals for 3 minutes for medium or until the sirloin is of the desired degree of doneness, turning frequently. Serve with black bean and rice salad.

SERVES 4

Note: *This dish may be prepared 1 day in advance and assembled by you or your guests just before grilling.*

Beer-Marinated Beef

1 (12-ounce) can beer
1 envelope onion soup mix
1 envelope brown gravy mix
2½ pounds stew meat
⅓ cup flour

Combine the beer, soup mix and gravy mix in a slow cooker and mix well. Combine the stew meat and flour in a sealable plastic bag, tossing to coat. Add the contents of the bag to the slow cooker and mix gently to coat the stew meat with the liquid mixture. Cook, covered, on Low for about 8 hours. Serve with hot cooked noodles, rice or mashed potatoes.

SERVES 8 TO 10
Note: *May substitute one cubed round steak for the stew meat.*

Pompano Beach Air Park is the winter home of the Goodyear Blimp Base.

Bourbon Chili

2 pounds ground beef
½ cup chopped onion
2 (16-ounce) cans whole tomatoes
2 (16-ounce) cans red beans or kidney beans
½ cup bourbon
¼ cup chili powder
¼ cup vinegar
2 teaspoons salt

Brown the ground beef with the onion in a large saucepan, stirring until the ground beef is crumbly; drain. Stir in the undrained tomatoes, undrained beans, bourbon, chili powder, vinegar and salt. Simmer for 2 to 2½ hours or until of the desired consistency, stirring occasionally.

SERVES 6

Reuben Meat Loaf

1½ to 2 pounds ground round
½ medium onion, chopped
1 teaspoon Dijon mustard
1 teaspoon garlic salt
1 teaspoon freshly ground pepper
1 teaspoon Worcestershire sauce
1 (8-ounce) bottle Russian salad dressing
6 slices rye bread, torn
2 eggs, lightly beaten
1 (8-ounce) can sauerkraut, drained
1 cup shredded Swiss cheese

Combine the ground round, onion, Dijon mustard, garlic salt, pepper and Worcestershire sauce in a bowl and mix well. Add ½ cup of the Russian dressing, rye bread and eggs and mix until the mixture forms a ball.

Pat the ground round mixture into a rectangle on a sheet of waxed paper. Spread the sauerkraut over the rectangle; sprinkle with the cheese. Roll into a loaf, pinching the ends to seal. Place in a baking dish.

Bake at 350 degrees for 40 to 55 minutes or until brown and cooked through. Drizzle the top of the meat loaf with the remaining Russian dressing. Bake for 5 minutes longer. Let stand for 5 minutes before serving.

SERVES 4 TO 6

Picadillo

3 pounds ground beef
6 medium yellow onions, chopped
4 green bell peppers, chopped
2 red bell peppers, chopped
3 (28-ounce) cans crushed tomatoes
2 jars large capers, drained
1 (15-ounce) package raisins
1 (6-ounce) jar pimento-stuffed green olives, drained
   Hot cooked rice

Brown the ground beef in a stockpot, stirring until crumbly; drain. Sauté the onions, green peppers and red peppers in a nonstick skillet for 5 minutes or until tender-crisp. Add the onion mixture, undrained tomatoes and capers to the stockpot.

Simmer, covered, for 1 hour and 50 minutes, stirring occasionally. Add the raisins and olives. Simmer for 10 minutes longer. Spoon over hot cooked rice.

SERVES 10 TO 12

Note: *This recipe can easily be cut in half, but it is even better the next day!*

Taco Quiche

1	unbaked (10-inch) deep-dish pie shell
1	pound ground beef
1	envelope taco seasoning mix
2	jalapeños, chopped (optional)
2	cups shredded Colby Longhorn cheese
2	cups shredded Monterey Jack cheese
1	cup milk
4	eggs, lightly beaten

Bake the pie shell at 350 degrees for 10 minutes. Let stand until cool. Brown the ground beef in a skillet, stirring until crumbly; drain. Stir in the taco seasoning mix. Add the jalapeños and mix well.

Sprinkle 1 cup of the Colby Longhorn cheese and 1 cup of the Monterey Jack cheese over the bottom of the pie shell. Spread with the ground beef mixture. Sprinkle with the remaining Colby Longhorn cheese and Monterey Jack cheese. Pour a mixture of the milk and eggs over the top. Bake at 350 degrees for 45 minutes or until set and golden brown.

SERVES 8

Note: *Serve with sour cream and guacamole if desired.*

Bourbon Pork

¼	cup Dijon mustard
¼	cup packed brown sugar
¼	cup bourbon
¼	cup chopped scallions
¼	cup soy sauce
	Chopped fresh rosemary to taste
1	pork tenderloin

Combine the Dijon mustard, brown sugar, bourbon, scallions, soy sauce and rosemary in a bowl and mix well. Pour over the pork tenderloin in a dish, turning to coat. Marinate, covered, in the refrigerator for 8 to 10 hours, turning occasionally. Drain, reserving the marinade. Bring the reserved marinade to a boil in a saucepan. Boil for 2 minutes. Place the tenderloin in a roasting pan. Bake at 350 degrees or grill over hot coals until cooked through, basting with the cooked marinade occasionally.

SERVES 2

Note: *May substitute any cut of pork for the tenderloin.*

Pork Loin Fillets with Bourbon Glaze

4	**(6- to 8-ounce) pork loin fillets**
1	**tablespoon cracked pepper**
1	**tablespoon olive oil**
2	**shallots, minced**
8	**ounces mixed wild mushrooms**
2	**tablespoons balsamic vinegar**
1	**cup beef stock**
1/4	**cup bourbon**
1	**tablespoon chopped fresh thyme**
1/2	**cup whipping cream**
1	**tablespoon cornstarch**
1	**tablespoon water**
1	**tablespoon green peppercorns**

Coat the fillets with the cracked pepper. Sear the fillets on both sides in an ovenproof skillet in 1½ teaspoons of the olive oil. Bake at 400 degrees for 8 to 10 minutes or until cooked through, turning once.

Heat the remaining 1½ teaspoons olive oil in a saucepan. Add the shallots. Cook until light brown, stirring constantly. Stir in the mushrooms and balsamic vinegar. Cook over medium-high heat until most of the liquid has been absorbed, stirring frequently.

Add the stock, bourbon and thyme. Cook until reduced by half, stirring frequently; strain. Stir in the whipping cream. Bring to a boil. Add a mixture of the cornstarch and water. Cook until thickened, stirring constantly. Stir in the peppercorns. Drizzle the sauce over the fillets.

SERVES 4

Pork Medallions with Sautéed Apples

1	**(1-pound) pork tenderloin**
3/4	**cup bread crumbs**
3/4	**cup grated Parmesan cheese**
1	**egg, beaten**
1	**tablespoon water**
1/4	**cup flour**
1/4	**cup plus 1 tablespoon butter**
2	**large Red or Golden Delicious apples, peeled, sliced**
4	**shallots, chopped**
	Salt and pepper to taste
1/4	**cup canned chicken broth**

Cut the tenderloin diagonally into ½-inch slices. Pound ⅛ inch thick between sheets of waxed paper with a meat mallet. Mix the bread crumbs and cheese in a shallow dish. Whisk the egg and water in a bowl. Coat the tenderloin with the flour, shaking off the excess. Dip in the egg. Coat with the bread crumb mixture. Heat ¼ cup of the butter in a heavy skillet over medium heat. Add the tenderloin in batches.

Cook for 3 minutes per side or until light brown and cooked through. Remove to a platter with a slotted spoon, reserving the pan drippings. Cover to keep warm.

Add the remaining 1 tablespoon butter to the reserved pan drippings. Heat over medium heat until the butter melts. Add the apples and shallots and mix well. Sauté for 5 minutes or until tender. Season with salt and pepper. Stir in the broth. Simmer for 5 minutes or until of a syrupy consistency, stirring occasionally. Arrange the tenderloin on a serving platter. Spoon the apple mixture around the tenderloin. Serve immediately.

SERVES 4

Photograph for this recipe appears on page 78.

Orange Pork Steaks

6   **blade or arm pork steaks (about 2½ pounds)**

       Salt to taste

4   **medium sweet potatoes, cut into ½-inch slices**

1   **medium orange, thinly sliced**

       Juice of 1 orange

½   **cup packed brown sugar**

⅛   **teaspoon each salt, cinnamon and nutmeg**

Trim the excess fat from the steaks. Render the trimmings in a skillet, reserving 1 tablespoon of the drippings. Discard the trimmings. Cook the steaks in the reserved drippings just until brown on both sides. Sprinkle with salt.

Layer the sweet potatoes and 1 sliced orange in a 9x13-inch baking dish. Top with the steaks. Combine the orange juice with enough water to measure ½ cup. Combine the orange juice mixture, brown sugar, salt, cinnamon and nutmeg in a bowl and mix well. Pour over the layers. Bake, covered, at 350 degrees for 45 minutes; remove cover. Bake for 30 minutes longer or until cooked through.

SERVES 6

The Bonnet House, a historic site near Fort Lauderdale Beach, was named for the Bonnet Lilies found in the waters on the property.

Sausage-Stuffed Eggplant

2   **(1¼-pound) eggplant**

1   **pound Italian sausage, casings removed**

1   **tablespoon vegetable oil**

4   **ounces mushrooms, sliced**

¾   **cup chopped carrot**

½   **cup freshly grated Parmesan cheese**

Cut the eggplant lengthwise into halves. Remove the pulp, leaving a ¼-inch shell. Chop the pulp. Arrange the shells in an 8x12-inch baking dish. Brown the sausage in a skillet, stirring until crumbly; drain. Wipe the skillet with a paper towel. Heat the oil in the skillet until hot. Stir in the eggplant pulp, mushrooms and carrot.

Sauté until tender. Stir in the sausage and cheese. Spoon the eggplant mixture into the shells. Bake at 375 degrees for 15 to 20 minutes or until heated through.

SERVES 4

Note: *Substitute your favorite cheese for the Parmesan cheese if desired.*

Bleu Cheese Veal Chops

¾ cup dry white wine

1 large shallot, minced

1 cup whipping cream

4 ounces bleu cheese, crumbled

Salt and black pepper to taste

½ teaspoon cayenne

½ teaspoon thyme

½ teaspoon garlic powder

¼ teaspoon white pepper

¼ teaspoon black pepper

¼ teaspoon salt

4 (9-ounce) veal chops

Olive oil

Bring the white wine and shallot to a boil in a saucepan over high heat. Boil for 5 minutes or until the mixture is reduced by half. Strain, discarding the shallot. Return the liquid to the saucepan. Whisk in the whipping cream and bleu cheese. Bring to a boil.

Boil for 10 minutes or until the mixture is reduced to ¾ cup and of a sauce consistency, stirring occasionally. Season with salt and black pepper to taste. Remove from heat. Cover to keep warm.

Mix the cayenne, thyme, garlic powder, white pepper, ¼ teaspoon black pepper and ¼ teaspoon salt in a bowl. Brush both sides of the veal chops with olive oil and coat with the spice mixture. Grill the veal chops over hot coals for 4 minutes per side for medium-rare or until of the desired degree of doneness. Arrange 1 veal chop on each dinner plate. Drizzle with the bleu cheese sauce.

May prepare the sauce in advance and store, covered, in the refrigerator. Reheat just before serving.

SERVES 4

Veal in Madeira and Caper Sauce

6 veal cutlets

Flour

White pepper to taste

Italian seasoning to taste

Butter

½ cup madeira

½ cup whipping cream

1 tablespoon capers

Salt and black pepper to taste

Hot cooked rice or pasta

Coat the cutlets on both sides with a mixture of flour, white pepper and Italian seasoning. Sauté in butter in a skillet until brown on both sides. Remove the cutlets to a platter, reserving the pan drippings. Cover to keep warm.

Stir the wine into the reserved pan drippings. Add the whipping cream, capers, salt and black pepper and mix well. Cook until of the desired consistency, stirring constantly. Arrange the cutlets over the rice or pasta on a serving platter. Drizzle with the wine sauce.

SERVES 4

Arroz con Pollo

1   (2½- to 3-pound) chicken, cut
     into quarters
     Salt, pepper and oregano to taste
     Vegetable oil
1   large onion, chopped
2   cups water
1   cup rice
2   medium tomatoes, chopped
⅛   teaspoon saffron

Sprinkle the chicken with salt, pepper and oregano. Sauté the chicken in oil in a skillet until brown on all sides. Remove the chicken with a slotted spoon to a platter, reserving the pan drippings.

Sauté the onion in the reserved pan drippings until tender. Add the chicken, water and rice and mix well. Stir in the tomatoes and saffron. Simmer until the rice is tender and the chicken is cooked through, stirring occasionally.

SERVES 4 TO 6

Spicy Grilled Chicken with Pineapple Salsa

½   pineapple, coarsely chopped
1   large onion, chopped
1   or 2 jalapeños, seeded, minced
1   tablespoon chopped fresh cilantro
1   teaspoon fresh lime juice
1   teaspoon red wine vinegar
⅛   teaspoon salt
1   head garlic, minced
2   tablespoons vegetable oil
1   (3-pound) chicken, cut up
1½   teaspoons paprika
1½   teaspoons thyme
1½   teaspoons oregano
¾   teaspoon cayenne
½   teaspoon salt
¼   teaspoon ground black pepper

Mix the pineapple, onion, jalapeños, cilantro, lime juice, wine vinegar and ⅛ teaspoon salt in a bowl. Let stand at room temperature for 6 to 8 hours to allow the flavors to marry before serving.

Combine the garlic and oil in a shallow dish and mix well. Add the chicken, tossing to coat. Mix the paprika, thyme, oregano, cayenne, ½ teaspoon salt and black pepper in a bowl. Sprinkle over both sides of the chicken and pat lightly.

Grill the chicken over hot coals for 25 to 30 minutes or until cooked through, turning 1 or 2 times. Serve immediately with pineapple salsa.

SERVES 4 TO 5

Note: *May substitute 3 pounds chicken breasts for the whole chicken. Don't enjoy grilling? Bake at 350 degrees for approximately 1 hour or until the chicken is cooked through.*

Southwest Chicken Bake

1   (2½-pound) chicken, poached
2   (4-ounce) cans green chiles
2   cups sour cream
1   medium onion, chopped
16 ounces Cheddar cheese, shredded
16 ounces Monterey Jack cheese, shredded
1   teaspoon garlic powder
    Salt and pepper to taste
4   small cans enchilada sauce
1   (2-ounce) package small corn tortillas
½   cup vegetable oil, heated or melted butter

Chop the chicken, discarding the skin and bones. Combine the chicken, chiles, sour cream, onion, half the Cheddar cheese, half the Monterey Jack cheese, garlic powder, salt and pepper in a bowl and mix well.

Grease a 9x13-inch baking dish. Spread the bottom with just enough of the enchilada sauce to cover. Dip the tortillas in the oil and then in the enchilada sauce. Spoon some of the chicken mixture in the center of each tortilla. Roll to enclose the filling.

Arrange the tortillas seam side down in the prepared dish, allowing the tortillas to touch. Sprinkle with the remaining Cheddar cheese and Monterey Jack cheese. Bake at 350 degrees for 45 minutes.

SERVES 4

Chicken Avocado Melt

4   boneless skinless chicken breast halves
2   tablespoons cornstarch
1   teaspoon cumin
1   teaspoon garlic salt
1   egg, lightly beaten
1   tablespoon water
⅓   cup yellow cornmeal
3   tablespoons vegetable oil
1   ripe avocado, sliced
1½ cups shredded Monterey Jack cheese
½   cup sour cream
¼   cup sliced green onion tops
¼   cup chopped red bell pepper

Pound the chicken ¼ inch thick between sheets of plastic wrap. Mix the cornstarch, cumin and garlic salt in a shallow dish. Add the chicken, tossing to coat.

Whisk the egg and water in a bowl. Dip the chicken in the egg mixture and coat with the cornmeal. Heat the oil in a skillet over medium heat until hot. Add the chicken.

Cook for 2 minutes on each side, turning once. Remove the chicken to a baking pan. Arrange the avocado over the chicken. Sprinkle with the cheese. Bake at 350 degrees for 15 minutes or until the chicken is cooked through and the cheese is bubbly. Transfer the chicken to a serving platter. Top with the sour cream and sprinkle with the green onion tops and red pepper.

SERVES 2 TO 4

Chicken Asparagus Crepes

1   **pound boneless skinless chicken breasts**

1   **pound asparagus spears, trimmed**

2   **tablespoons butter**

¼   **cup flour**

2   **cups milk**
     Salt and pepper to taste
     Tabasco sauce to taste

8   **ounces Swiss cheese, shredded**
     Crepes

Cut the chicken into thin strips. Combine the chicken with enough water to cover in a saucepan. Bring to a boil; reduce heat. Cook for 15 to 20 minutes or until the chicken is tender; drain. Cover to keep warm. Combine the asparagus with enough water to cover in a saucepan. Bring to a boil; reduce heat. Cook until the asparagus is tender-crisp; drain. Cover to keep warm.

Heat the butter in a saucepan until melted. Add the flour and mix well. Cook for 1 minute, stirring constantly. Add the milk ½ cup at a time. Cook after each addition until thickened, stirring constantly. Season with salt, pepper and Tabasco sauce. Add ¾ of the cheese, stirring until blended. Simmer, covered, over low heat to keep warm.

Arrange some of the chicken, several of the asparagus spears, some of the sauce and some of the remaining cheese in the center of each crepe. Roll to enclose the filling. Arrange in a dish. Drizzle with the remaining sauce. Serve immediately.

SERVES 10

Crepes

1½   **cups flour**

1   **tablespoon sugar**

½   **teaspoon baking powder**

⅛   **teaspoon salt**

2   **cups milk**

2   **eggs**

2   **tablespoons melted butter**
     Melted butter

Mix the flour, sugar, baking powder and salt in a mixer bowl. Add the milk, eggs and 2 tablespoons butter. Beat at medium speed for 2 minutes. Chill, covered, in the refrigerator.

Brush the bottom of an 8-inch crepe pan with melted butter. Pour ¼ cup of the chilled crepe batter into the pan, tilting to spread evenly. Cook for 1 minute. Loosen the side of the crepe with a spatula and turn. Cook for 1 minute longer or until golden brown. Repeat the process with the remaining batter.

Chicken with Tomato and Feta Cheese

4   whole chicken breasts, split
    Salt and pepper to taste
2   tablespoons olive oil
3   large shallots, chopped
2   teaspoons oregano
2   cups undrained canned crushed
    tomatoes
1   (15-ounce) can low-sodium
    chicken broth
1   cup crumbled feta cheese
1/3 cup chopped black olives

Sprinkle the chicken with salt and pepper. Heat the olive oil in a heavy skillet over medium-high heat until hot. Add the shallots and oregano. Sauté for 5 minutes or until the shallots are tender. Add the chicken and mix well. Sauté for 7 minutes per side. Stir in the tomatoes and broth. Bring to a boil; reduce heat. Simmer over medium-low heat for 10 minutes or just until the chicken is cooked through, stirring occasionally.

Transfer the chicken with a slotted spoon to a serving platter. Boil the remaining tomato mixture over high heat for 5 minutes or until thickened, stirring frequently. Stir in the feta cheese and black olives. Return the chicken to the saucepan. Simmer for 5 minutes, stirring occasionally.

SERVES 4

A colony of Brazilian squirrel monkeys has occupied the Bonnet House estate in Fort Lauderdale for many years. In fact, they can be seen jumping overhead at the main gate at any given time of day.

Chinese Chicken

4   boneless chicken breasts
1   cup flour
3   tablespoons butter
3/4 cup soy sauce, or to taste
1/2 cup sugar
1   large onion, sliced
1/2 to 3/4 cup cooking sherry

Coat the chicken with the flour. Sauté in the butter in a skillet for 5 minutes per side, turning once. Add the soy sauce, sugar, onion and sherry to the skillet and mix well. Simmer for 30 to 45 minutes or until the chicken is cooked through, turning occasionally.

SERVES 4

Note: *Serve with yellow rice and beans of your choice.*

Lemon Chicken

2   **boneless chicken breast halves**
    Salt and pepper to taste
1   **tablespoon butter**
1   **tablespoon olive oil**
8   **ounces mushrooms, thinly sliced**
4   **cloves of garlic, chopped**
8   **paper-thin slices lemon**
½   **cup dry white wine**
2   **tablespoons fresh lemon juice**
    Chopped fresh parsley

Sprinkle the chicken on both sides with salt and pepper. Heat the butter and olive oil in a heavy skillet over high heat until the butter melts. Add the chicken. Sauté for 2 minutes per side. Transfer the chicken with a slotted spoon to a platter, reserving the pan drippings.

Sauté the mushrooms and garlic in the reserved pan drippings for 4 minutes or until the mushrooms are tender. Return the chicken to the skillet. Overlap 4 lemon slices on each piece of chicken. Pour the white wine and lemon juice around the chicken.

Simmer, covered, over low heat for 5 minutes or until the chicken is cooked through; remove cover. Simmer for 5 minutes longer or until the sauce is reduced and slightly thickened, stirring frequently. Season with salt and pepper. Transfer the chicken to 2 dinner plates. Spoon the sauce around the chicken. Sprinkle with the parsley.

SERVES 2

Pecan Chicken Breasts with Mustard Sauce

4   **boneless skinless chicken breast**
    halves
    Salt and pepper to taste
¼   **cup butter**
2   **tablespoons Dijon mustard**
6   **ounces pecans, chopped**
¼   **cup butter**
2   **tablespoons safflower oil**
½   **cup sour cream**
2   **tablespoons Dijon mustard**
1   **teaspoon salt**

Pound the chicken between sheets of waxed paper until flattened. Sprinkle with salt and pepper to taste. Heat ¼ cup butter in a saucepan over medium heat. Remove from heat. Whisk in 2 tablespoons Dijon mustard. Dip the chicken in the butter mixture. Coat with the pecans.

Heat ¼ cup butter and safflower oil in a heavy skillet until hot. Sauté the chicken in batches in the butter mixture for 5 minutes per side; do not crowd the chicken. Remove the chicken to a baking pan with a slotted spoon. Keep warm in a 200-degree oven. Discard the pan drippings, reserving the pecans. Discard any burnt pecans. Spoon reserved pecans over the chicken.

Deglaze the skillet with the sour cream, scraping up any browned bits. Whisk in 2 tablespoons Dijon mustard, 1 teaspoon salt and pepper. Remove from heat. Spoon some of the sour cream sauce in the middle of each of 4 heated dinner plates. Top with the chicken. Serve immediately.

SERVES 4

Smoked Mozzarella Chicken Breasts

4   (4-ounce) boneless skinless
    chicken breasts

½   cup bread crumbs

1½ tablespoons chopped fresh thyme,
    or ¾ teaspoon dried thyme

½   teaspoon paprika

½   teaspoon freshly ground pepper

2½ ounces smoked mozzarella cheese,
    coarsely chopped

1   small bunch fresh basil (about
    30 leaves)
    Marsala Sauce

Pound the chicken ¼ inch thick between sheets of waxed paper with a wooden mallet. Mix the bread crumbs, thyme, paprika and pepper on a piece of foil. Coat both sides of the chicken with the bread crumb mixture.

Arrange ¼ of the cheese and ¼ of the basil in the center of each chicken breast. Roll to enclose the filling. Arrange seam side down in a nonstick baking dish. Bake at 375 degrees for 30 minutes or until the chicken is cooked through. Serve with Marsala Sauce.

SERVES 4

From 1939 to 1979, Stranahan House was partially converted into four different restaurants—The Egret, Casa Basque, Swiss Chalet, and—the oldest and most popular—Pioneer Restaurant.

Marsala Sauce

8   ounces mushrooms, sliced

2   tablespoons chopped shallots

3   tablespoons butter

3   tablespoons flour

½   cup dry marsala

¼   cup water

1   tablespoon parsley flakes

¼   teaspoon rosemary, crushed

Sauté the mushrooms and shallots in the butter in a skillet until tender. Sprinkle with the flour. Cook for 3 to 4 minutes, stirring frequently. Stir in the wine, water, parsley flakes and rosemary. Bring to a boil; reduce heat. Simmer for 3 to 4 minutes or until thickened, stirring frequently.

Spinach-Stuffed Chicken Breasts

1   tablespoon vegetable oil

1   onion, finely chopped

2   cloves of garlic, finely chopped

3   cups chopped cooked spinach, drained

2   tablespoons chopped fresh parsley

2   tablespoons chopped fresh basil, or 1 teaspoon dried basil

1   cup ricotta cheese

1   cup shredded mozzarella cheese

1/2 cup grated Parmesan cheese

1   egg, lightly beaten

1/2 teaspoon salt
     Freshly ground pepper to taste

6   boneless chicken breast halves (about 2 pounds)

Heat the oil over medium heat until hot. Add the onion and garlic. Cook until the onion is tender, stirring frequently. Remove from heat. Stir in the spinach, parsley and basil. Let stand until cool. Combine the ricotta cheese, mozzarella cheese, Parmesan cheese, egg, salt and pepper in a bowl. Stir in the spinach mixture.

Arrange the chicken breasts skin side up on a hard surface. Loosen the skin from 1 side of each chicken breast to form a pocket. Spoon 1/6 of the spinach mixture into each pocket. Press gently on the surface of the skin to spread the mixture evenly. Tuck the ends of the skin and meat under each chicken breast to form a dome shape. Arrange in a greased baking dish.

Bake at 375 degrees for 35 minutes or until the skin is golden brown and the juices run clear. Serve immediately.

SERVES 6

Note: *May serve chilled for variety.*

Swiss Chicken

6   boneless chicken breast halves

9   slices Swiss cheese

1   (10-ounce) can cream of chicken soup

1/2 cup white wine
     Salt and pepper to taste
     Bread crumbs

1/4 cup melted butter

Arrange the chicken in a single layer in a baking pan. Top each chicken breast with 1½ slices of the cheese. Pour a mixture of the soup and white wine over the chicken. Sprinkle with salt, pepper and bread crumbs. Drizzle with the butter. Bake at 350 degrees for 1 hour or until the chicken is cooked through.

SERVES 6

Birds of Paradise

4	boneless skinless chicken breast halves
2	eggs, lightly beaten
1	cup grated Parmesan cheese (not fresh)
1	tablespoon butter
1	cup white wine
1	cup sliced mushrooms

Cut the chicken into 1-inch-thick strips. Dip in the eggs and coat with the cheese. Brown the chicken on all sides in the butter in a skillet. Add the wine and mushrooms.

Sauté for 5 minutes. Spoon the chicken mixture into a nonstick baking dish. Bake, covered, at 350 degrees for 45 to 60 minutes or until the chicken is cooked through.

SERVES 4

Chicken Paprika

¾	cup vegetable juice cocktail
2	teaspoons paprika
1½	teaspoons flour
½	teaspoon seasoned salt
1	teaspoon olive oil
½	cup sliced green onions with tops
1	clove of garlic, minced
8	ounces boneless skinless chicken breasts, cut into 2-inch strips
2	tablespoons sour cream
	Fresh parsley, snipped
1	cup hot cooked rice

Mix the vegetable juice cocktail, paprika, flour and seasoned salt in a bowl. Heat the olive oil in a skillet over medium heat. Add the green onions and garlic. Cook for 1 minute, stirring constantly. Add the chicken and mix well.

Cook until the chicken is light brown, stirring constantly. Stir in the vegetable juice mixture. Bring to a boil, stirring frequently; reduce heat.

Simmer, covered, over low heat for 15 minutes or until the chicken is cooked through, stirring occasionally. Remove from heat. Stir in the sour cream. Sprinkle with the parsley. Spoon over the hot cooked rice on 3 dinner plates.

SERVES 3

Chicken Tortilla Casserole

6	boneless skinless chicken breast halves
1/2	cup thinly sliced green onions
1	clove of garlic, minced
2	tablespoons vegetable oil
4	cups cold chicken broth
3	tablespoons cornstarch
1	cup shredded Monterey Jack cheese
1/2	cup mayonnaise-type salad dressing
1/2	cup sour cream
1	(4-ounce) can chopped green chiles
1/4	cup sliced black olives
1/4	cup chopped fresh cilantro or parsley
12	(6-inch) flour tortillas
1/4	cup sliced black olives
1/2	cup shredded Monterey Jack cheese

Cut the chicken into thin strips. Sauté the chicken, green onions and garlic in the oil in a skillet until the chicken is light brown and cooked through.

Mix the broth and cornstarch in a saucepan. Bring to a boil, stirring constantly. Boil for 1 minute. Remove from heat. Stir in 1 cup cheese, salad dressing, sour cream, undrained chiles, 1/4 cup black olives and cilantro. Combine 1 cup of the sauce with the chicken mixture in a bowl and mix well.

Spoon some of the chicken mixture in the center of each tortilla. Roll to enclose the filling. Arrange seam side down in a nonstick 9x13-inch baking pan. Spoon the remaining sauce over the tortillas. Sprinkle with 1/4 cup black olives and 1/2 cup cheese. Bake at 350 degrees for 25 minutes or until heated through.

SERVES 6

On December 5, 1945, five Avenger torpedo bombers took off from the Fort Lauderdale Naval Air Station (which is now Fort Lauderdale-Hollywood International Airport) carrying fifteen men on a training mission. A distress call was received, saying, "We seem to be off course." They were never seen again, and no trace of the planes was ever found. This strange incident was the first to mark the area now known as the Bermuda Triangle.

Chicken Kabobs

1½   **cups vegetable oil**

¾   **cup soy sauce**

½   **cup red wine**

⅓   **cup lemon juice**

¼   **cup Worcestershire sauce**

2   **tablespoons dry mustard**

1   **tablespoon pepper**

2   **teaspoons salt**

1½   **teaspoons parsley flakes**

2   **cloves of garlic, crushed**

2   **pounds boneless skinless chicken breasts, cut into pieces**

     Mushrooms

     Pearl onions

     Red and/or green bell peppers, sliced

Combine the oil, soy sauce, red wine, lemon juice, Worcestershire sauce, dry mustard, pepper, salt, parsley flakes and garlic in a nonreactive bowl and mix well. Add the chicken, tossing to coat.

Marinate, covered, in the refrigerator for 24 hours or longer; drain. Thread the chicken, mushrooms, pearl onions and bell peppers alternately on skewers until all of the ingredients are used. Grill over hot coals until the chicken is cooked through, turning frequently.

SERVES 6

Note: *May substitute shrimp or beef for the chicken.*

Roasted Cornish Game Hens

2   **Cornish game hens, cleaned**

     Salt to taste

2   **Granny Smith apples, peeled, cut into thin wedges**

1   **package dried pitted prunes**

     Mango chutney (optional)

Sprinkle the inside cavity of each game hen lightly with salt. Stuff the apples and prunes into each cavity. Place each game hen breast side up in a deep baking pan.

Roast at 350 degrees for 40 minutes. Brush with the chutney. Roast for 20 minutes longer or until cooked through. Remove from oven. Cut the game hens from neck to tail into halves with poultry shears. Arrange each half stuffing side up on a dinner plate.

SERVES 4

Vegetable-Stuffed Turkey Loaf

1   cup chopped broccoli
1/3   cup chopped red bell pepper
2   to 3 tablespoons water
2   tablespoons grated Parmesan cheese
1/2   cup fine dry bread crumbs
1/2   cup finely chopped onion
1/4   cup milk
1   egg, lightly beaten
1/2   teaspoon thyme, crushed
1/4   teaspoon rosemary, crushed
1/4   teaspoon garlic salt
1/4   teaspoon pepper
1 1/2 pounds ground turkey
2   tablespoons currant jelly, melted

Combine the broccoli, red pepper and water in a microwave-safe dish. Microwave on High for 2 to 3 minutes or until the vegetables are tender-crisp; drain. Stir in the cheese.

Combine the bread crumbs, onion, milk, egg, thyme, rosemary, garlic salt and pepper in a bowl and mix well. Add the turkey and mix well. Pat the turkey mixture into an 8x12-inch rectangle on a sheet of waxed paper. Spread the broccoli mixture over the rectangle to within 1 inch of the edges. Roll from the short end using the waxed paper to lift the mixture and peeling the waxed paper away as you roll. Place in a loaf pan.

Bake at 350 degrees for 1 to 1 1/4 hours or until the loaf is cooked through. Transfer to a serving platter. Brush the loaf with the jelly.

SERVES 6

Nobel Prize-winning novelist Ernest Hemingway made Key West his home from 1931 to 1939. There he wrote To Have and Have Not (which takes place in Key West), Death in the Afternoon, and the beginning of For Whom The Bell Tolls. The island celebrates Hemingway Days in July.

Dolphinfish Divine

1½ **pounds dolphinfish or mahimahi fillets**

½ **cup flour**

1 **egg, lightly beaten**

2 **tablespoons water**

3 **to 4 tablespoons butter**

½ **cup white wine**

¼ **cup butter**

1 **cup sliced mushrooms**

1 **teaspoon lemon juice**

5 **fresh artichokes, trimmed, sliced**

½ **cup chopped green onions**

Coat the fillets with the flour. Dip in a mixture of the egg and water. Sauté the fillets in 3 to 4 tablespoons butter in a skillet over medium heat for 10 minutes.

Add the white wine, ¼ cup butter, mushrooms, lemon juice and artichokes to the skillet. Sauté for 1 minute. Sprinkle with the green onions. Serve immediately.

SERVES 4

Note: *May substitute canned artichoke hearts for the fresh artichokes.*

Zesty Broiled Dolphinfish

2 **dolphinfish fillets**

Lemon or lime juice

Zesty Seafood Sauce

Marinate the fillets in lemon or lime juice in a nonreactive dish for 5 minutes. Arrange the fillets on a rack in a broiler pan. Broil for 8 minutes; turn the fillets.

Spread with Zesty Seafood Sauce. Broil for 3 to 5 minutes longer or until the fish flakes easily and the sauce is heated through.

SERVES 2

Note: *May substitute grouper or any white fish for the dolphinfish.*

Zesty Seafood Sauce

½ **cup grated Parmesan cheese**

¼ **cup butter or margarine, softened**

2 **tablespoons mayonnaise**

2 **tablespoons chopped onion**

½ **teaspoon (about) Worcestershire sauce**

Combine the cheese, butter, mayonnaise, onion and Worcestershire sauce in a bowl and mix well.

Floribbean Grouper

¼   teaspoon minced garlic

2   (10-ounce) cans tomatoes with green chiles

3   tomatoes, chopped

1   onion, chopped

1   each red and green bell pepper, chopped

3   basil leaves, finely chopped

10   pine nuts, lightly toasted

½   cup chopped fresh cilantro

½   cup chopped green onions

1   teaspoon nutmeg

¼   teaspoon minced garlic

     Salt and pepper to taste

2   carrots, sliced, steamed

2   pounds grouper fillets

½   cup flour

     Hot cooked angel hair pasta

Sauté ¼ teaspoon garlic in a nonstick skillet for 2 minutes. Stir in the undrained canned tomatoes with green chiles, tomatoes, onion, red pepper, green pepper, basil and pine nuts. Simmer for 1 hour, stirring occasionally.

Sauté the cilantro, green onions, nutmeg, ¼ teaspoon garlic, salt and pepper in a skillet for 5 minutes. Add the carrots and mix well. Sauté for 5 minutes longer.

Coat the grouper lightly with the flour. Heat a skillet sprayed with nonstick cooking spray over high heat until hot; reduce heat to medium. Place the grouper in the skillet. Cook for 5 to 7 minutes or until the grouper flakes easily. Remove from heat.

Spoon the pasta onto a serving platter. Arrange the grouper over the pasta. Top with the sautéed vegetable mixtures.

SERVES 4

Grilled Grouper Medley

2   tablespoons butter

2   medium yellow squash, sliced

2   medium red bell peppers, chopped

1   medium zucchini, sliced

1   medium onion, chopped

3   medium tomatoes, cut into wedges

½   cup butter

2   pounds grouper fillets

½   cup soy sauce

4   ounces feta cheese, crumbled

     Garlic salt and pepper to taste

Heat 2 tablespoons butter in a skillet until melted. Sauté the yellow squash, red peppers, zucchini and onion in the butter for 5 minutes.

Spoon the sautéed vegetables and tomatoes in the center of a 16x34-inch sheet of foil. Dot with ½ cup butter. Arrange the grouper over the vegetables. Drizzle with the soy sauce. Sprinkle with the feta cheese, garlic salt and pepper. Fold the foil to enclose and seal the edges.

Grill the foil packet over hot coals for 15 minutes; pierce the foil with a fork. Turn the packet over and pierce again. Grill for 15 minutes longer or until the grouper flakes easily. May substitute dolphinfish for the grouper.

SERVES 4 TO 6

Snapper with Black Bean and Corn Salsa

2   tablespoons olive oil
4   (6-ounce) red or yellowtail
     snapper fillets
     Black Bean and Corn Salsa

Heat the olive oil in a nonstick skillet over high heat. Add the fish. Cook for 3 to 5 minutes per side or until brown and crisp. Transfer to dinner plates. Spread some of the Black Bean and Corn Salsa over each fillet.

SERVES 4

The first barbecue? Juan Ortiz, a Spanish soldier, escaped a fiery death by the Timucuan Indians that they called "barbacoa," or "barbecue" in English—something to think about when you grill your next steak.

Black Bean and Corn Salsa

1   **(16-ounce) can black beans, drained, rinsed**
1   **cup fresh or frozen whole kernel corn**
1   **cup chopped red onion**
1   **medium green bell pepper, chopped**
3   **tablespoons wine vinegar**
3   **tablespoons olive oil**
1   **teaspoon lime juice**
     Salt and pepper to taste

Mix the beans, corn, onion, green pepper, wine vinegar, olive oil and lime juice in a bowl. Season with salt and pepper. Let stand, covered, at room temperature for 1 hour. May be prepared in advance and stored, covered, in the refrigerator. Bring to room temperature before serving.

Note: *Great served over grilled swordfish or dolphinfish.*

Captain Bill's Baby Snapper Fillets

2	tomatoes, peeled, thinly sliced
¾	cup seasoned bread crumbs
	Salt and pepper to taste
1½	small red snapper fillets
	Wine Sauce
½	cup freshly grated Parmesan cheese
	Paprika to taste

Arrange the tomato slices in 4 buttered gratin dishes. Sprinkle 3 tablespoons of the bread crumbs over the tomatoes in each dish. Season with salt and pepper. Layer some of the red snapper in each dish. Drizzle with the Wine Sauce. Sprinkle each serving with 2 tablespoons of the cheese. Top with paprika. Bake at 500 degrees for 10 minutes.

SERVES 4

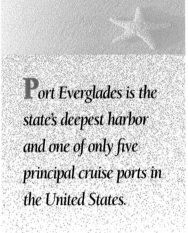

Port Everglades is the state's deepest harbor and one of only five principal cruise ports in the United States.

Wine Sauce

½	cup white port
¼	cup butter
1	teaspoon Key lime juice

Combine the wine, butter and lime juice in a saucepan. Cook over low heat until the butter melts, stirring frequently. Bring to a boil over medium heat. Boil for 3 minutes, stirring frequently.

Photograph for this recipe appears on page 78.

Grilled Tuna with Tomato Basil Vinaigrette

6   (8-ounce) tuna steaks
¼   cup virgin olive oil
¼   cup dry white wine
1   tablespoon minced garlic
     Salt and freshly ground pepper
     to taste
     Tomato Basil Vinaigrette

Arrange the steaks in a single layer in a nonreactive dish. Whisk the olive oil, white wine, garlic, salt and pepper in a bowl. Pour over the steaks, turning to coat. Marinate, covered, at room temperature for 1 hour or up to 6 hours in the refrigerator. Drain, reserving the marinade. Bring the reserved marinade to a boil in a saucepan. Boil for 2 minutes.

Grill the steaks over hot coals for 5 to 7 minutes or until the steaks flake easily, basting with the cooked reserved marinade occasionally. Drizzle with the Tomato Basil Vinaigrette.

SERVES 6

Note: *Serve with Asparagus with Parsley Vinaigrette on page 122.*

½   cup virgin or light olive oil
4   medium tomatoes, peeled, seeded,
     chopped
¼   cup finely chopped red onion
¼   cup minced fresh basil
¼   cup finely chopped drained
     sun-dried tomatoes
¼   cup drained small capers
1   teaspoon minced garlic
½   teaspoon salt
½   teaspoon freshly ground pepper

Tomato Basil Vinaigrette

Combine the olive oil, tomatoes, onion, basil, sun-dried tomatoes, capers, garlic, salt and pepper in a bowl and mix gently.

Note: *The vinaigrette may be prepared 1 day in advance and stored, covered, in the refrigerator, adding the basil and salt just before serving.*

104

Yellowtail Snapper with Onions

5	large red onions, sliced,
2	tablespoons olive oil
1/2	cup packed brown sugar
1/3	cup balsamic vinegar
3	tablespoons butter
	Salt and pepper to taste
4	yellowtail snapper fillets
2	tablespoons olive oil
	Madeira Sauce

Separate the onion slices into rings. Sauté the onions in 2 tablespoons olive oil in a skillet until dark brown and caramelized. Add the brown sugar and vinegar and mix well. Cook until the vinegar is absorbed. Stir in the butter, salt and pepper.

Sprinkle the fillets with salt and pepper. Sauté in 2 tablespoons olive oil in an ovenproof skillet until light brown. Bake at 350 degrees until the fillets flake easily. Spoon several tablespoons of the Madeira Sauce in the center of each dinner plate. Arrange 1 fillet on each plate. Top with the caramelized onions.

SERVES 4

Madeira Sauce

1	shallot, minced
1/4	cup butter
1/4	cup madeira
1	tablespoon lemon juice
3/4	cup whipping cream
	Salt and pepper to taste

Sauté the shallot in the butter in a saucepan until tender. Stir in the wine and lemon juice. Cook until reduced slightly, stirring frequently. Add the whipping cream, salt and pepper and mix well. Simmer for 30 minutes, stirring occasionally.

Key Lime Coconut Curry Sauce

2/3	cup canned cream of coconut
1/2	cup Key lime juice
7	tablespoons minced green onions
2	teaspoons curry powder
1/2	teaspoon cayenne
1/2	teaspoon salt
1/4	teaspoon freshly ground black pepper

Whisk the cream of coconut and lime juice in a bowl. Stir in the green onions, curry powder, cayenne, salt and black pepper. Chill, covered, in the refrigerator. Brush the sauce over fresh Florida seafood before and during the grilling process. Be sure to reserve some of the sauce to serve with the seafood.

MAKES 1 1/2 CUPS

Note: *May substitute fresh lime juice for the Key lime juice. May be prepared 1 day in advance and stored, covered, in the refrigerator.*

Florida Crab Cakes with Mayonnaise Caper Sauce

1   pound backfin lump crab meat
1   egg, lightly beaten
2   tablespoons mayonnaise
1½ tablespoons chopped fresh parsley
1   tablespoon Worcestershire sauce
1½ teaspoons dry mustard
⅛   teaspoon (heaping) sage
⅛   teaspoon (heaping) thyme
    Salt and pepper to taste
½   to 1 cup cracker meal
    Vegetable oil for frying
    Mayonnaise Caper Sauce

Combine the crab meat, egg, mayonnaise, parsley, Worcestershire sauce, dry mustard, sage, thyme, salt and pepper in a bowl and mix well. Add the cracker meal, mixing until the mixture adheres. Shape into patties. Chill for 1 hour or longer.

Fry the patties in hot oil in a skillet until brown on both sides; drain. Serve with Mayonnaise Caper Sauce.

SERVES 4

Robin redbreasts only visit Florida in the winter and occasionally make a meal of red berries of the Brazilian pepper. They become so intoxicated that they can sometimes be seen staggering across lawns.

Mayonnaise Caper Sauce

1   cup mayonnaise
2   tablespoons drained capers
1   teaspoon horseradish
½   teaspoon dillweed
½   teaspoon finely chopped fresh parsley
½   teaspoon red wine vinegar

Mix the mayonnaise, capers, horseradish, dillweed, parsley and wine vinegar in a bowl. Chill, covered, in the refrigerator.

Note: *The flavor of the sauce is enhanced if prepared 1 day in advance and stored, covered, in the refrigerator.*

Florida Clambake

Lettuce leaves

4 Florida lobster tails, split

12 clams in shells, scrubbed

4 ears of corn in husks

8 small red potatoes, cut into halves

1 cup melted salted or unsalted butter

1 envelope onion soup mix

2 cloves of garlic, crushed

2 teaspoons oregano

Cut 4 large sheets of foil. Spread lettuce leaves in the center of each sheet. Arrange 1 lobster tail, 3 clams, 1 ear of corn and 4 potato halves over the lettuce. Brush with a mixture of the butter, soup mix, garlic and oregano.

Fold the foil loosely to enclose and seal the edges. Grill over medium-hot coals for 20 to 30 minutes or until the clams open.

SERVES 4

Photograph for this recipe appears on page 78.

Rum-Glazed Scallops

12 large cloves of garlic, cut into halves

20 large sea scallops

Salt and pepper to taste

2 tablespoons butter

¼ cup dark rum

¼ cup orange juice

¼ cup dry Champagne

3 tablespoons chopped shallots

3 tablespoons chopped fresh chives

2 tablespoons butter

Combine the garlic with enough water to cover in a saucepan. Bring to a boil; drain. Return the garlic to the saucepan. Add water to cover. Bring to a boil; drain.

Sprinkle the scallops with salt and pepper. Sauté in 2 tablespoons butter in a skillet over high heat for 3 minutes per side or until tender. Transfer the scallops to a platter using tongs, reserving the pan drippings. Tent with foil to keep warm.

Stir the garlic, rum and orange juice into the reserved pan drippings. Bring to a boil. Boil for 3 minutes or until of the consistency of a glaze, stirring frequently. Add the Champagne, shallots and 2 tablespoons of the chives and mix well.

Boil for 4 minutes or until reduced and of a sauce consistency, stirring frequently. Whisk in 2 tablespoons butter until melted. Season with salt and pepper. Drizzle over the scallops. Sprinkle with the remaining 1 tablespoon chives.

SERVES 4

Shrimp Chardonnay

1   **pound large shrimp**
4   **large cloves of garlic**
1/2   **cup extra-virgin olive oil**
1/2   **cup white chardonnay**
1/2   **cup chicken broth**
1/4   **cup butter**
1   **tablespoon chopped fresh parsley**
     Juice of 1 lemon
1   **cup seasoned Italian bread crumbs**
     Lemon wedges

Peel and devein the shrimp, leaving the tails intact. Sauté the garlic in the olive oil in an ovenproof skillet until golden brown. Add the shrimp, wine, broth, butter, parsley and lemon juice.

Sauté until the shrimp are almost cooked through. Sprinkle with the bread crumbs. Broil until the bread crumbs are brown. Serve with lemon wedges.

SERVES 4

Note: *Serve over hot cooked rice if desired.*

Shrimp Pie

1   **onion, chopped**
1   **cup chopped celery**
1/2   **green bell pepper, chopped**
1/2   **cup butter or margarine**
2   **cups cooked shrimp**
2   **cups cooked white rice**
1   **(10-ounce) can tomato soup**
1 1/2 **cups shredded Cheddar cheese**
1   **tablespoon Worcestershire sauce**
     Salt and pepper to taste
     Tabasco sauce to taste
1 1/2 **cups shredded Cheddar cheese**

Sauté the onion, celery and green pepper in the butter in a skillet until tender. Combine the sautéed vegetables, shrimp, rice, soup, 1 1/2 cups cheese and Worcestershire sauce in a bowl and mix well. Season with salt, pepper and Tabasco sauce.

Spoon the shrimp mixture into a greased 2-quart baking dish. Bake at 350 degrees for 20 to 25 minutes or until heated through. Sprinkle with 1 1/2 cups cheese. Bake for 15 minutes longer.

SERVES 8

Szechwan Spiced Shrimp

1	pound shrimp
2	tablespoons flour
1	tablespoon cornstarch
¼	teaspoon salt
¼	teaspoon baking soda
1	egg, lightly beaten
1	teaspoon dry sherry
1	teaspoon thin soy sauce
2	scallions with tops, finely chopped
2	or 3 dried chile peppers, finely chopped
2	teaspoons minced garlic
1	teaspoon finely minced gingerroot
3	tablespoons sugar
3	tablespoons catsup
5	teaspoons black soy sauce
1	tablespoon water
2	teaspoons pale dry sherry
1	teaspoon white vinegar
2	cups vegetable oil
1	teaspoon sesame oil

Peel and devein the shrimp. Cut the shrimp horizontally into halves. Combine the flour, cornstarch, salt and baking soda in a bowl and mix well. Stir in the egg, 1 teaspoon sherry and 1 teaspoon soy sauce. Add the shrimp, stirring to coat. Chill for 1 hour or longer, stirring occasionally.

Mix the scallions, chile peppers, garlic and gingerroot in a bowl. Combine the sugar, catsup, 5 teaspoons soy sauce, water, 2 teaspoons sherry and vinegar in a bowl and mix well.

Heat the vegetable oil in a wok over medium heat. Add half the shrimp mixture. Stir-fry for 10 seconds or until the shrimp turn whitish-pink. Remove the shrimp to a bowl with a slotted spoon. Repeat the process with the remaining shrimp mixture.

Discard all but 2 tablespoons of the pan drippings. Heat the reserved pan drippings in the wok until hot. Add the scallion mixture and mix well. Stir-fry until light brown. Add the catsup mixture and mix well.

Cook until the mixture begins to bubble, stirring frequently. Return the shrimp to the wok. Stir-fry for several seconds. Swirl in the sesame oil. Spoon onto dinner plates.

SERVES 2 TO 4

Sponsored by

JUNIOR LEAGUE OF GREATER FORT LAUDERDALE, INC.

Shrimp and Linguini with Sherry Cream Sauce

3	tablespoons butter or margarine
1	pound medium shrimp, peeled, deveined
1	tablespoon chopped garlic
2	teaspoons chopped shallots
6	tablespoons cream sherry
1	cup whipping cream
3	tablespoons chopped fresh parsley
	Salt and freshly ground pepper to taste
8	ounces linguini, cooked al dente, drained
3	radicchio leaves (optional)
3	lemon slices (optional)
	Sprigs of parsley (optional)

Heat the butter in a large skillet over medium heat until melted. Increase the heat to medium-high. Add the shrimp, garlic and shallots. Sauté for 15 to 20 seconds. Stir in the cream sherry. Add the whipping cream, parsley, salt and pepper and mix well.

Cook until the shrimp turn pink, stirring constantly. Remove the shrimp with a slotted spoon to a bowl. Cover to keep warm. Cook the sauce until reduced by $1/4$ to $1/2$ depending on the desired consistency, stirring constantly.

Return the shrimp to the skillet. Cook just until heated through, stirring constantly. Spoon the hot pasta onto 3 dinner plates. Divide the shrimp evenly between the servings. Drizzle with the sauce. Top each serving with a radicchio leaf, a lemon slice and parsley.

SERVES 3

Photograph for this recipe appears on page 116.

Shrimp Fettuccini

1   onion, chopped

1   green bell pepper, chopped

1   teaspoon garlic

1/2 cup butter

1   pound shrimp, peeled, deveined

1   (10-ounce) can cream of mushroom soup

1   medium block mild or hot Velveeta cheese, chopped

16 ounces fettuccini, cooked, drained

Sauté the onion, green pepper and garlic in the butter in a skillet. Add the shrimp and mix well.

Cook for 10 minutes, stirring frequently. Stir in the soup. Cook for 2 minutes, stirring frequently. Add the cheese. Cook until the cheese melts, stirring constantly. Spoon over the pasta on a serving platter.

SERVES 6

Note: *Add the desired amount of canned tomatoes with chiles to add a little zing.*

Vegetable Spaghetti

6   chicken bouillon cubes

1/2 cup hot water

2   red bell peppers, chopped

2   yellow bell peppers, chopped

1   large onion, chopped

2   tablespoons olive oil

1/2 cup chopped fresh cilantro

2   cloves of garlic, minced

2   (16- to 20-ounce) cans peeled tomatoes with basil

12 to 14 plum tomatoes, cut into quarters

16 ounces spaghetti, cooked, drained

Dissolve the bouillon cubes in the hot water and mix well. Sauté the red peppers, yellow peppers and onion in the olive oil in a skillet. Add the cilantro and garlic and mix well. Stir in the undrained canned tomatoes, plum tomatoes and bouillon.

Simmer for 2 hours, stirring occasionally. Toss with the hot pasta in a bowl. Serve immediately.

SERVES 4

Tortellini Prosciutto

16 ounces tortellini

8 ounces prosciutto or pancetta, julienned

1 tablespoon olive oil

1 tablespoon butter

1 shallot, minced

1 clove of garlic, minced

1 (15-ounce) can crushed tomatoes

2/3 cup chicken broth

5 tablespoons tomato paste

6 basil leaves, julienned

Salt and pepper to taste

1/2 cup freshly grated fontina cheese

Cook the pasta using package directions; drain. Cover to keep warm. Sauté the prosciutto in a mixture of the olive oil and butter in a large skillet over medium-high heat. Stir in the shallot and garlic. Sweat, covered, until tender. Stir in the undrained tomatoes, broth and tomato paste.

Simmer for 3 to 5 minutes, stirring frequently. Add the basil, salt and pepper and mix well. Add the pasta and toss to mix. Cook just until heated through, stirring frequently. Spoon onto a serving platter. Sprinkle with the cheese.

SERVES 4

Frank and Ivy Stranahan, early pioneers and visionaries of Fort Lauderdale (then called the "New River"), used to entertain such affluent guests as Mr. and Mrs. Henry Flagler and Mr. and Mrs. William Brickell.

SEA
SIDES

VEGETABLES AND
SIDE DISHES

Sponsored by

ELIZABETH WINBORNE WOLTZ
and
ELIZABETH WINBORNE WOLTZ

Asparagus with Parsley Vinaigrette

¼   cup red wine vinegar

¼   cup minced fresh parsley

1   tablespoon Dijon mustard

1   teaspoon sugar

½   teaspoon salt

½   teaspoon ground pepper

½   cup olive oil

1   pound fresh asparagus spears,
    steamed

Whisk the wine vinegar, parsley, Dijon mustard, sugar, salt and pepper in a bowl. Whisk in the olive oil gradually. Arrange the hot or chilled asparagus on a serving platter. Drizzle with the vinaigrette.

SERVES 4

During World War II, Winston Churchill paid a visit to the Lighthouse Point area and dined at Cap's Place.

Asparagus with Pine Nuts

1   pound asparagus spears, trimmed

1   medium Vidalia onion, sliced

1   tablespoon chopped garlic

1   tablespoon lemon butter oil

½   cup pine nuts, toasted

    Salt and pepper to taste

Cut the asparagus spears into bite-size pieces. Fill a medium skillet with water to measure ½ inch. Add the asparagus.

Steam, covered, for 5 minutes or until tender-crisp; drain. Add the onion, garlic and lemon butter oil.

Sauté until the onion is tender. Stir in the pine nuts, salt and pepper.

SERVES 4

Note: *Serve over hot cooked pasta for a meatless entrée.*

OVERLEAF: *Clockwise from top left: Black Beans and Rice, Palm Polenta, Garden Vegetable Ribbons, Floribbean Sweet Potato Timbales*

122

Black Beans and Rice

2   cups canned black beans, drained,
     rinsed
2   cups cooked rice
1½   cups chopped fresh cilantro
¾   cup olive oil
¼   cup Key lime juice
½   cup chopped red onion
3   cloves of garlic, minced
     Salt and freshly ground pepper
     to taste

Mix the black beans, rice and cilantro in a bowl. Whisk the olive oil into the lime juice in a bowl. Stir in the onion and garlic. Add to the bean mixture and mix well. Season with salt and pepper.

SERVES 6

Note: *The flavor is enhanced if prepared 1 day in advance and stored, covered, in the refrigerator. May substitute cooked dried black beans for the canned black beans. Great way to use leftover black beans and rice.*

Photograph for this recipe appears on page 120.

Green Beans with Bacon

2   (16-ounce) cans green beans
8   slices bacon
2   tablespoons vinegar
2   teaspoons sugar
½   teaspoon salt
¼   teaspoon garlic powder
⅛   teaspoon pepper

Heat the green beans in a saucepan until hot; drain. Cover to keep warm. Fry the bacon in a skillet until crisp. Drain, reserving ¼ cup of the drippings. Crumble the bacon.

Combine the reserved drippings, vinegar, sugar, salt, garlic powder and pepper in a saucepan and mix well. Add the green beans. Cook just until the green beans are coated and heated through, stirring frequently. Spoon into a serving bowl. Sprinkle with the bacon.

SERVES 6 TO 8

Lemon Couscous with Spinach

2¼   cups chicken broth

¼   cup butter

     Kosher salt to taste

1   (10-ounce) package couscous

     Lemon juice to taste

1   small bunch spinach, trimmed

3   tablespoons thinly sliced green
     onions

3   tablespoons chopped chives
     (optional)

Bring the chicken broth, butter and salt to a boil in a saucepan. Stir in the couscous. Remove from heat. Let stand, covered, for 5 minutes.

Fluff the couscous with a fork. Stir in the lemon juice, spinach, green onions and chives.

SERVES 6 TO 8

Eggplant-Stuffed Red Peppers

8   red bell peppers

1   large unpeeled eggplant, chopped

¼   cup olive oil

1   (7-ounce) jar Stoned Gaeta black
     olives

3   to 4 cloves of garlic, finely
     chopped

1   (4-ounce) jar capers, drained,
     chopped

3   anchovies, chopped

     Salt and pepper to taste

     Oregano to taste

     Bread crumbs

Arrange the red peppers on a broiler rack. Broil until the outer skin is blistered and charred on all sides, turning frequently; do not burn. Place the red peppers in a sealable plastic bag. Let stand until cool. Peel, core and seed the red peppers, being careful to leave the peppers intact.

Sauté the eggplant lightly in half the olive oil; drain. Sauté the olives, garlic, capers, anchovies, salt, pepper, oregano and enough bread crumbs to hold the mixture together in the remaining olive oil in a skillet. Stir in the eggplant. Spoon the mixture into the red peppers. Arrange on a baking sheet. Bake at 375 degrees for 30 minutes.

SERVES 4

Cheesy Vidalia Onion Casserole

5	or 6 Vidalia onions, sliced
1/2	cup melted butter or margarine
	Grated Parmesan cheese to taste
3/4	cup butter cracker crumbs
3/4	cup cheese cracker crumbs
	Salt and pepper to taste
1	(10-ounce) can cream of mushroom soup
1	cup shredded Cheddar cheese
	Paprika to taste

Sauté the onions in the butter in a skillet until tender. Layer the onions, Parmesan cheese, butter cracker crumbs, cheese cracker crumbs, salt and pepper 1/2 at a time in a 1 1/2-quart baking dish. Spread with the soup. Sprinkle with the Cheddar cheese, Parmesan cheese and paprika. Bake at 350 degrees for 30 minutes.

SERVES 6

Las Olas Boulevard was the first road to the beach in Fort Lauderdale in 1917.

Baked Pineapple Surprise

2	(20-ounce) cans juice-pack chunk pineapple
1	cup diced American cheese
3/4	cup sugar
2	tablespoons flour
6	slices bread, cubed
1/2	cup melted butter

Drain the pineapple, reserving 1 cup of the juice. Spread the pineapple over the bottom of a buttered 9x13-inch baking pan. Top with the cheese. Sprinkle with a mixture of the sugar and flour. Drizzle with the reserved pineapple juice. Toss the bread cubes with the butter in a bowl. Arrange over the top. Bake at 350 degrees for 45 minutes.

SERVES 6 TO 8

Tropical Baked Pineapple

1   loaf bread

3   eggs

2   cups sugar

½   cup butter, cubed

½   cup whipping cream

1   (20-ounce) can crushed pineapple

Tear enough bread into ½-inch pieces to measure 1 quart. Whisk the eggs in a bowl until blended. Stir in the sugar and butter. Add the whipping cream and undrained pineapple and mix well. Fold in the bread.

Spoon the pineapple mixture into a 9x11-inch or round baking dish. Bake at 350 degrees for 45 minutes or until brown and bubbly.

SERVES 6 TO 8

Note: *This is a great recipe to make use of that dried or frozen bread that always seems to be around.*

Palm Polenta

2½   cups canned low-sodium chicken broth

1½   cups water

1   cup polenta

1   cup grated Parmesan cheese

¼   cup sour cream

2   tablespoons butter or margarine

     Salt and freshly ground pepper to taste

1   (14-ounce) can hearts of palm, drained, sliced lengthwise

     Shredded coconut

Combine the broth, water and polenta in a saucepan and mix well. Bring to a boil, stirring constantly. Reduce heat to low. Simmer for 15 minutes or until thickened.

Add the cheese, sour cream and butter to the polenta and mix well. Season with salt and pepper. Spoon into a serving bowl. Top with the hearts of palm and coconut.

SERVES 8 TO 10

Note: *May substitute coarsely ground yellow cornmeal for the polenta and fat-free sour cream for the sour cream.*

Photograph for this recipe appears on page 120.

Floribbean Sweet Potato Timbales

3   **pounds sweet potatoes or yams, peeled, cut into chunks**

¼   **cup freshly squeezed Florida orange juice**

¼   **cup packed light brown sugar**

¼   **cup butter or margarine**

1½   **tablespoons Grand Marnier**

1   **tablespoon finely grated fresh orange peel**

½   **teaspoon cinnamon**

¼   **teaspoon nutmeg**

⅛   **teaspoon ginger**

2   **eggs, lightly beaten**

¼   **cup freshly grated coconut**

       Tropical Fruit Salsa

Combine the sweet potatoes with enough boiling water to cover in a saucepan. Cook for 20 to 30 minutes or until tender; drain.

Combine the sweet potatoes, orange juice, brown sugar, butter, liqueur, orange peel, cinnamon, nutmeg and ginger in a bowl. Mash until smooth. Add the eggs, stirring until blended. Spoon into a greased 2-quart square baking dish. Bake at 350 degrees for 45 minutes.

Make the timbales by oiling a small deep cup. Spoon the warm sweet potato mixture into the cup and press lightly; smooth the top. Run a small knife around the inside of the cup and invert onto individual plates or a platter. (If one of the timbales falls apart, return the mixture to the cup and try again.) Garnish top and sides of timbales with the coconut and Tropical Fruit Salsa.

SERVES 8 TO 10

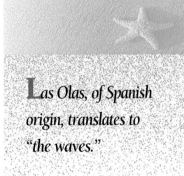

L*as Olas, of Spanish origin, translates to "the waves."*

Tropical Fruit Salsa

1   **ripe mango, chopped**

1   **ripe papaya, chopped**

1   **ripe plum or nectarine, chopped**

2   **kiwifruit, chopped**

2   **tablespoons freshly squeezed Florida orange juice**

Mix the mango, papaya, plum, kiwifruit and orange juice in a bowl.

Photograph for this recipe appears on page 120.

Sweet Potato Soufflé

1 (29-ounce) can sweet potatoes, drained
1½ cups sugar
1 cup evaporated milk
2 eggs, lightly beaten
2 tablespoons margarine, softened
1 teaspoon cinnamon
1 cup packed brown sugar
2 tablespoons melted margarine
1 cup chopped pecans
¾ cup crushed cornflakes

Mash the sweet potatoes in a bowl. Stir in the sugar, evaporated milk, eggs, 2 tablespoons softened margarine and cinnamon. Spoon into a baking pan sprayed with nonstick cooking spray. Bake at 350 degrees for 45 minutes or until firm.

Mix the brown sugar and 2 tablespoons melted margarine in a bowl. Stir in the pecans and cornflakes. Spread over the baked layer. Bake for 15 minutes longer.

SERVES 7

Cheesy Potato Casserole

1 (32-ounce) package frozen hash brown potatoes
1 (10-ounce) can cream of chicken soup
2 cups shredded Cheddar cheese
2 cups sour cream
1 cup grated onion
2 teaspoons Tabasco sauce
1 teaspoon salt
½ teaspoon pepper
2 cups crushed cornflakes
¼ cup melted butter

Reserve ¼ of the hash brown potatoes for another use. Combine the remaining hash brown potatoes, soup, cheese, sour cream, onion, Tabasco sauce, salt and pepper in a bowl and mix well. Spoon into a greased baking dish.

Mix the cornflakes and butter in a bowl. Spread over the potato mixture. Bake at 350 degrees for 1 hour.

SERVES 6 TO 8

Grilled Potatoes

2   cups chopped peeled potatoes
1   cup thinly sliced carrot
1/2   cup chopped celery
2   tablespoons water
1   cup chopped onion
1/2   teaspoon salt
1/2   teaspoon pepper
2   tablespoons butter
8   slices crisp-fried bacon

Combine the potatoes, carrot, celery and water in a microwave-safe dish. Microwave for 3 minutes; stir. Microwave for 3½ to 5 minutes. Stir in the onion; drain. Add the salt and pepper and mix well.

Layer 2 sheets of heavy-duty foil on a hard surface. Spoon the potato mixture in the center of the foil. Dot with the butter. Arrange the bacon over the top. Seal the foil to enclose the mixture.

Grill the foil packet over hot coals for 25 to 30 minutes or until the vegetables are of the desired degree of crispness.

SERVES 6

Note: *May cook the vegetables in a saucepan over medium heat for 5 minutes.*

The three Seminole Indian reservations in Florida are Big Cypress, Brighton, and Hollywood.

Twice-Baked Potatoes

6   medium potatoes, baked
      Melted butter
3/4   cup milk
1/2   cup sour cream
1/2   cup (or more) favorite shredded cheese
1/4   cup butter, softened
      Bacon bits

Cut the potatoes lengthwise into halves. Scoop the pulp into a bowl, leaving the shells intact. Coat the inside of the shells lightly with melted butter. Arrange the shells on a baking sheet. Heat in a 350-degree oven.

Add the milk, sour cream, cheese and ¼ cup butter to the potato pulp and mix with a fork. The mixture may be somewhat lumpy. Add additional milk, sour cream or butter if desired. Spoon into the heated potato shells. Sprinkle with bacon bits. Bake for 10 to 15 minutes or until bubbly. Serve immediately.

SERVES 12

Mexican Rice

⅔ **cup rice**

¼ **cup chopped onion**

1 **clove of garlic, crushed**

2 **tablespoons olive oil**

2 **cups hot water**

½ **cup chopped fresh cilantro**

¼ **cup chopped tomatoes with green chiles**

2 **tablespoons tomato sauce**

2 **tablespoons chopped jalapeños**

1 **teaspoon salt**

Pepper to taste

Lime slices (optional)

Sour cream

Sauté the rice, onion and garlic in the olive oil in a skillet until light brown. Stir in the hot water, cilantro, tomatoes with green chiles, tomato sauce, jalapeños, salt and pepper. Bring to a boil; reduce heat.

Simmer, covered, for 20 to 30 minutes or until the liquid is absorbed and the rice is tender. Serve with lime slices and/or sour cream.

SERVES 4

Spanakopita (Spinach Pie)

2 **all ready pie pastries**

2 **or 3 spring onions, finely sliced**

1 **teaspoon butter**

1 **(10-ounce) package frozen spinach, thawed, drained**

10 **ounces feta cheese, crumbled**

½ **cup chopped fresh cilantro**

3 **eggs, lightly beaten**

2 **tablespoons finely chopped fresh dillweed**

1 **teaspoon nutmeg**

1 **teaspoon olive oil**

Salt and pepper to taste

1 **egg, beaten (optional)**

2 **tablespoons water (optional)**

Fit 1 of the pie pastries into a 9-inch pie plate. Bake using package directions for 5 to 6 minutes or until light brown.

Sauté the spring onions in the butter in a skillet until tender. Combine the spring onions, spinach, feta cheese, cilantro, 3 eggs, dillweed, nutmeg, olive oil, salt and pepper in a bowl and mix well. Spoon into the baked pie shell.

Top with the remaining pastry, fluting the edge and cutting vents. Brush with a mixture of 1 egg and the water. Bake at 350 degrees for 1 hour.

SERVES 5 TO 6

Squash and Tomato Bake

2	pounds yellow squash, sliced
1	cup water
2	(15-ounce) cans stewed tomatoes
1	tablespoon flour
2	teaspoons sugar
1	teaspoon salt
1	teaspoon paprika
$^1/_2$	teaspoon garlic powder
$^1/_8$	teaspoon pepper
$^1/_8$	teaspoon basil
2	cups shredded mozzarella cheese
$^1/_4$	to $^1/_2$ cup grated Parmesan cheese

Combine the squash and water in a saucepan. Bring to a boil. ...ce heat. Simmer, covered, for 10 minutes or until the squash is tender, stirring occasionally; drain.

Drain the tomatoes, reserving $^1/_4$ cup of the juice. Combine the reserved juice, tomatoes, flour, sugar, salt, paprika, garlic powder, pepper and basil in a saucepan and mix well. Bring to a boil; reduce heat. Simmer for 5 minutes, stirring occasionally. Remove from heat.

Layer half the squash, $^1/_4$ of the tomato mixture, 1 cup of the mozzarella cheese and $^1/_4$ of the remaining tomato mixture in a 2-quart baking dish sprayed with nonstick cooking spray. Continue layers with the remaining squash, remaining tomato mixture and remaining mozzarella cheese. Sprinkle with the Parmesan cheese. Bake at 350 degrees for 30 minutes. Let stand for 10 minutes before serving.

SERVES 6 TO 8

Note: *May sprinkle the Parmesan cheese over the top 5 minutes before the end of the cooking process. The top will not be crusty.*

Baked Tomatoes

3	or 4 large beefsteak tomatoes
4	ounces cream cheese
2	tablespoons butter
1	tablespoon chopped green onions
10	ounces spinach, cooked, drained
$^1/_4$	cup bread crumbs
	Sliced white creamy cheese (Havarti or mozzarella), cut into halves

Cut the tomatoes into $^1/_4$-inch slices. Arrange in a single layer on a broiler rack sprayed with nonstick cooking spray.

Heat the cream cheese, butter and green onions in a saucepan over low heat until mixed, stirring frequently. Stir in the spinach and bread crumbs. Spoon a large spoonful of the spinach mixture in the center of each tomato slice. Top with $^1/_2$ slice of cheese.

Bake at 350 degrees for 20 minutes or until bubbly. Serve immediately.

SERVES 6 TO 8

Italian Zucchini Casserole

2	pounds zucchini, thinly sliced lengthwise
1	cup ricotta cheese or low-fat ricotta cheese
2	eggs, lightly beaten
2	tablespoons grated Parmesan cheese
2	tablespoons skim milk
1/2	teaspoon pepper
3/4	cup shredded mozzarella cheese
2	tablespoons grated Parmesan cheese
1	can olive oil and garlic pasta sauce
1/4	cup chopped green onions
1	clove of garlic, minced
1/2	teaspoon whole basil

Arrange the zucchini on a broiler rack sprayed with nonstick cooking spray. Broil 3 inches from the heat source for 2 minutes or until brown; turn. Broil until brown. Combine the ricotta cheese, eggs, 2 tablespoons Parmesan cheese, skim milk and pepper in a bowl and mix well.

Layer 1/3 of the zucchini in a 7x11-inch baking dish sprayed with nonstick cooking spray. Spread with 1/2 of the ricotta cheese mixture and 1/2 cup of the mozzarella cheese. Top with 1/2 of the remaining zucchini, the remaining ricotta cheese mixture and the remaining 1/4 cup mozzarella cheese. Arrange the remaining zucchini over the prepared layers. Sprinkle with 2 tablespoons Parmesan cheese. Bake at 375 degrees for 30 minutes or until set and the top is golden brown.

Combine the pasta sauce, green onions, garlic and basil in a saucepan. Bring to a boil; reduce heat. Simmer for 10 minutes, stirring occasionally. Spread over the top of the baked layers.

SERVES 4 TO 6

Stranahan House in Fort Lauderdale, the oldest standing structure in Broward County, was built in 1901 as a trading post. It was converted into a home in 1906.

Rapid Ratatouille

5   **cups sliced zucchini**

1   **(28-ounce) can whole tomatoes, drained, coarsely chopped**

1½ **cups vertically sliced onions**

1   **cup green bell pepper strips**

1   **teaspoon Italian seasoning**

    Salt and pepper to taste

    Cumin to taste

    Grated Parmesan cheese (optional)

Combine the zucchini, tomatoes, onions, green pepper, seasoning, salt, pepper and cumin in a microwave-safe 2-quart dish and mix well.

Microwave, covered, on High for 7 minutes; stir. Microwave for 7 minutes longer. Serve with Parmesan cheese.

SERVES 6

Garden Vegetable Ribbons

3   **large carrots, peeled**

2   **medium zucchini**

2   **medium yellow squash**

2   **tablespoons olive oil**

1   **tablespoon butter or margarine, softened**

2   **tablespoons chopped fresh basil**

    Salt and freshly ground pepper to taste

    Fresh basil leaves

Draw a vegetable peeler down the full length of the carrots, zucchini and yellow squash to make thin strips.

Pour water to measure ½ inch into a saucepan. Bring to a boil. Add the carrots. Cook over medium heat for 2 to 3 minutes. Add the zucchini and yellow squash. Cook for 2 minutes longer; drain. Spoon into a serving bowl.

Add the olive oil, butter and basil to the vegetable mixture, tossing to coat. Season with salt and pepper. Top with fresh basil leaves.

SERVES 4 TO 6

Note: *Garden Vegetable Ribbons may be served alongside a rice, grain or pasta dish to add color. Four tablespoons commercial basil pesto may be used as a substitute for the oil, butter and basil.*

Photograph for this recipe appears on page 120.

SUN-KISSED SWEETS

DESERTS

Sponsored by

**LINDA ASKINAS, ROBIN DUNN,
LESLIE FLAVELL, MICHELLE KLOS,
LAURA LANG, CINDY MAHONEY,
JANE SMITH, CHRIS WELCH**

Amaretto Bread Pudding

1   **loaf French bread**

1   **quart half-and-half or evaporated skim milk**

2   **tablespoons unsalted butter, softened**

1½   **cups sugar**

3   **eggs**

2   **tablespoons almond extract**

¾   **cup golden raisins**

¾   **cup sliced almonds**

     Amaretto Sauce

Tear the bread into bite-size pieces into a bowl. Pour the half-and-half over the bread. Chill, covered, for 1 hour. Spread the butter over the bottom and up the sides of a 9x13-inch baking dish.

Beat the sugar, eggs and flavoring in a bowl until blended. Stir in the bread mixture. Fold in the raisins and almonds. Spoon into the prepared baking dish.

Set the baking dish on the middle oven rack. Bake at 325 degrees for 50 minutes or until golden brown. Cool in pan on a wire rack.

Cut the bread pudding into 8 to 10 squares and arrange on an ovenproof platter. Spoon the Amaretto Sauce over the squares. Broil until bubbly. Serve immediately.

SERVES 8 TO 10

Everglades National Park encompasses over 1.5 million acres, stretching more than sixty miles north to south and forty miles east to west.

Amaretto Sauce

1   **cup confectioners' sugar**

½   **cup unsalted butter, softened**

1   **egg, beaten**

¼   **cup amaretto**

Combine the confectioners' sugar and butter in a double boiler. Cook over simmering water until the confectioners' sugar dissolves and the mixture is very hot, stirring constantly. Remove from heat. Cool slightly.

Add the egg to the confectioners' sugar mixture, whisking constantly until the sauce cools to room temperature. Stir in the amaretto.

Note: *Double the sauce recipe for a more moist bread pudding.*

OVERLEAF: *Clockwise from left to right: Key Lime Tarts, KoKomo Trifle, Orange Balls, Raspberry Meringues with Apricot Sauce, My Favorite Chocolate Cake, Upside-Down Pineapple Cake*

Mascarpone Cheesecake

1/2   **cup graham cracker crumbs**

1/2   **cup ground almonds**

1/4   **cup melted butter**

32   **ounces cream cheese, softened**

2   **cups sugar**

1 1/2   **cups mascarpone cheese**

1   **cup sour cream**

2   **eggs**

2   **tablespoons orange juice**

1   **tablespoon vanilla extract**

Mix the graham cracker crumbs, almonds and butter in a bowl. Press the crumb mixture over the bottom and up the side of a buttered 9-inch springform pan.

Beat the cream cheese in a mixer bowl until creamy. Add the sugar, mascarpone cheese, sour cream and eggs. Beat for 5 minutes or until smooth, scraping the bowl occasionally. Add the orange juice and vanilla. Beat for 1 minute. Spoon into the prepared springform pan.

Bake at 350 degrees for 1 1/2 hours or until brown and set. Cool in pan on a wire rack. Chill, covered, for 4 hours or longer before serving.

SERVES 12

Note: *One-third cup sliced almonds, ground, is equivalent to one-half cup ground almonds.*

Praline Cheesecake

1 1/2   **cups graham cracker crumbs**

1/2   **cup melted butter**

1/2   **cup sugar**

1   **teaspoon cinnamon**

1   **teaspoon nutmeg**

32   **ounces cream cheese, softened**

3   **eggs**

1   **teaspoon vanilla extract**

2   **cups packed brown sugar**

1   **cup chopped pecans**

3   **tablespoons flour**

Combine the graham cracker crumbs, butter, sugar, cinnamon and nutmeg in a bowl and mix well. Press the crumb mixture over the bottom and up the side of a 9-inch springform pan.

Beat the cream cheese in a mixer bowl until smooth, scraping the bowl occasionally. Add the eggs and vanilla. Beat until fluffy. Add the brown sugar, pecans and flour, stirring just until combined. Spoon into the prepared pan. Bake at 350 degrees for 70 minutes. Cool in pan on a wire rack. Chill, covered, until serving time.

SERVES 12

Turtle Pecan Cheesecake

2   cups chocolate cookie crumbs or vanilla wafer crumbs (about 8 ounces)

¼   cup melted butter

20   ounces cream cheese, softened

1   cup sugar

1½ tablespoons flour

1   teaspoon vanilla extract

¼   teaspoon salt

3   eggs

2   tablespoons whipping cream

    Caramel Topping

    Chocolate Topping

1   cup chopped pecans, toasted

Mix the cookie crumbs and butter in a bowl. Press the crumb mixture over the bottom of a 9-inch springform pan.

Beat the cream cheese in a mixer bowl until creamy, scraping the bowl occasionally. Add the sugar, flour, vanilla and salt, beating until blended. Add the eggs 1 at a time, beating well after each addition. Blend in the whipping cream. Spoon into the prepared pan.

Bake at 450 degrees for 10 minutes. Reduce the oven temperature to 200 degrees. Bake for 35 to 40 minutes longer or until set. Loosen cheesecake from side of pan. Cool completely in pan on a wire rack. Remove the side of the pan.

Drizzle the cheesecake with Caramel Topping and Chocolate Topping. Chill, covered, in the refrigerator. Sprinkle with the pecans just before serving.

SERVES 8 TO 10

Birch State Park, located near Fort Lauderdale Beach and one of Broward County's oldest parks, was sold to the state for one silver dollar in 1942.

Caramel Topping

½ (14-ounce) package caramels

⅓ cup whipping cream

Combine the caramels and whipping cream in a saucepan. Cook over low heat until smooth, stirring frequently.

Chocolate Topping

4   ounces German's sweet chocolate

2   tablespoons whipping cream

1   teaspoon butter

Combine the chocolate, whipping cream and butter in a saucepan. Cook over low heat until smooth, stirring frequently.

Crème Brûlée

4   cups whipping cream

4   teaspoons vanilla extract

9   egg yolks, lightly beaten

1   cup sugar

½   teaspoon salt

¼   cup packed brown sugar

Heat the whipping cream and vanilla in a saucepan to a moderate temperature. Add a mixture of the egg yolks, sugar and salt gradually, stirring constantly. Spoon into 15 custard cups. Arrange the custard cups in a baking pan. Add enough hot water to reach halfway up the sides of the custard cups.

Bake at 325 degrees for 40 minutes or until a knife inserted in the centers come out clean. Remove the custard cups from the pan. Let stand until cool. Sprinkle the brown sugar lightly over the top of each serving. Arrange the custard cups on a baking sheet. Broil 6 inches from the heat source for 1 to 2 minutes or until the brown sugar is caramelized. Chill for 1 hour before serving.

SERVES 15

Note: *Award-winning recipe from On The Veranda Restaurant in Highlands, North Carolina.*

Frangipane Tart with Strawberries and Raspberries

1   all ready pie pastry

6   tablespoons unsalted butter, softened

½   cup sugar

¾   cup finely ground blanched almonds

1   tablespoon amaretto

1   tablespoon flour

1   egg

1   teaspoon almond extract

2   cups strawberries

2   cups raspberries

¼   cup strawberry or raspberry jam, melted, strained

Roll the pastry ⅛ inch thick on a lightly floured surface. Fit into a 10- or 11-inch round tart pan with a removable fluted side. Chill in the refrigerator.

Beat the butter and sugar in a mixer bowl until creamy, scraping the bowl occasionally. Add the almonds, amaretto, flour, egg and flavoring, beating until mixed. Spread evenly over the bottom of the chilled pastry. Bake on the middle oven rack at 375 degrees for 20 to 25 minutes or until the pastry is light golden brown. Cover loosely with foil if the frangipane begins to overbrown. Let stand until cool.

Cut the strawberries lengthwise into ⅛-inch slices. Arrange the strawberry slices overlapping with the raspberries in a decorative pattern over the top of the tart. Brush with the jam.

SERVES 10

Note: *May also top with sliced apples.*

Mango Cobbler

2¼   **cups baking mix**
⅓   **cup milk**
¾   **cup water**
¾   **cup packed brown sugar**
1½   **tablespoons cornstarch**
1   **teaspoon cinnamon**
½   **teaspoon nutmeg**
⅛   **teaspoon salt**
6   **cups sliced mangoes**

Combine the baking mix and milk in a bowl, mixing with a fork until moistened but lumpy.

Whisk the water, brown sugar, cornstarch, cinnamon, nutmeg and salt in a saucepan. Bring to a boil over high heat and whisk. Stir in the mangoes. Remove from heat.

Spoon the mango mixture into an 8x8-inch baking dish. Drop the baking mix mixture in mounds over the top.

Bake at 450 degrees for 20 minutes or until the crust is golden brown. Cool to room temperature. Serve with vanilla ice cream.

SERVES 12

One of the first to line up for Coral Springs land sales was well-known talk show host Johnny Carson.

Mocha Almond Fudge Girdlebuster

1¼   **cups graham cracker crumbs**
3   **tablespoons sugar**
⅓   **to ½ cup butter, softened**
1   **gallon vanilla ice cream, softened**
8   **Skor candy bars, broken**
1½   **cups flaked coconut**
½   **gallon mocha almond fudge ice cream, softened**
  Chocolate sauce

Mix the graham cracker crumbs, sugar and butter in a bowl. Press the crumb mixture over the bottom of a springform pan.

Layer ½ of the vanilla ice cream, 3 of the broken candy bars, ½ cup of the coconut, mocha almond fudge ice cream, 3 of the remaining broken candy bars, ½ cup of the remaining coconut, remaining vanilla ice cream, remaining broken candy bars and remaining coconut in the prepared pan.

Freeze, covered with plastic wrap, for 24 hours or longer. Top with the chocolate sauce just before serving.

SERVES 8

KoKomo Trifle

1¼ cups guava jelly

½ cup dark rum

¾ cup pineapple juice

¾ cup cream of coconut

1½ cups puréed strawberries

2 sponge cakes, torn into bite-size pieces

4 cups chopped mixed fruit (guava, pineapple, mango, papaya, passion fruit)

Orange Sauce

Sliced kiwifruit, star fruit, toasted coconut and/or sliced strawberries

Mix the jelly with ¼ cup of the rum in a saucepan. Heat until blended, stirring frequently. Combine the pineapple juice, cream of coconut and remaining ¼ cup rum in a bowl and mix well.

Layer the strawberry purée, sponge cakes, pineapple juice mixture, mixed fruit, guava jelly mixture and Orange Sauce ¼ at a time in a large glass serving bowl. Chill, covered, overnight. Top with sliced kiwifruit, sliced star fruit, toasted coconut and/or sliced strawberries just before serving.

SERVES 8 TO 10

Orange Sauce

¾ cup orange juice

½ cup sugar

¼ cup curaçao

8 egg yolks, lightly beaten

1 cup whipping cream

Combine the orange juice, sugar, curaçao and egg yolks in a double boiler and mix well. Cook until thickened, whisking constantly. Transfer to a bowl. Place in a larger bowl filled with ice water to reach halfway up the side of the smaller bowl. Whisk until chilled. Beat the whipping cream in a mixer bowl until soft peaks form. Fold into the chilled mixture. Chill, covered, in the refrigerator.

Photograph for this recipe appears on page 134.

Zabaglione Sauce

8 egg yolks

1 cup sugar

Juice of ½ lemon

⅛ teaspoon salt

1 cup sweet cream sherry

2 teaspoons brandy

1 cup whipping cream, whipped

Beat the egg yolks, sugar, lemon juice and salt in a mixer bowl until pale yellow. Transfer the mixture to a double boiler. Cook over hot water until thickened, stirring constantly. Remove from heat. Add the cream sherry and brandy gradually and mix well. Let stand until cool. Fold in the whipped cream. Serve with fresh raspberries or strawberries.

MAKES 3 TO 4 CUPS

143

Oranges in Grand Marnier

3   or 4 honeybell oranges or
     tangerines

1   cup sugar

1/2 cup water

1/2 cup Grand Marnier

1/4 teaspoon almond extract

Cut the oranges into decorative slices. Pack in a sterilized 1-quart jar. Combine the sugar and water in a saucepan. Bring to a boil over medium heat, stirring constantly. Boil for 1 minute. Remove from heat. Stir in the Grand Marnier and flavoring. Pour over the oranges, leaving a 1/2 inch headspace.

Cool slightly. Seal with 2-piece lids. Store in the refrigerator for up to 2 months. Reheat and serve over ice cream or pound cake.

MAKES 1 QUART

Note: *Stir into iced tea as a garnish as well as a sweetener.*

The Florida Everglades is actually a large, extremely shallow river, flowing very slowly from Lake Okeechobee southward to the sea. The Everglades is called "Pa-hay-oke," or "river of grass," by the Indians.

Orange Balls

1   (12-ounce) package vanilla wafers, crushed

1   cup confectioners' sugar

1   (6-ounce) can frozen orange juice concentrate

3/4 cup chopped nuts
     Confectioners' sugar

Combine the vanilla wafer crumbs, 1 cup confectioners' sugar, orange juice concentrate and nuts in a bowl and mix well. Shape into 1-inch balls. Roll in confectioners' sugar to coat.

SERVES 10

Photograph for this recipe appears on page 134.

144

Pumpkin Pecan Dessert with Caramel Sauce

1   (29-ounce) can pumpkin
1   cup sugar
1   (5-ounce) can evaporated milk
3   eggs, lightly beaten
2   teaspoons cinnamon
½   teaspoon salt
1   (2-layer) package pudding-recipe yellow cake mix
1½   cups finely chopped pecans
1   cup melted butter, cooled
1   cup whipping cream
1½   tablespoons confectioners' sugar
¾   teaspoon vanilla extract
     Caramel Sauce

Line two 9-inch round baking dishes with waxed paper. Combine the pumpkin, sugar, evaporated milk, eggs, cinnamon and salt in a bowl and mix well. Spoon into the prepared baking dishes. Sprinkle with the cake mix and pecans. Drizzle with the butter. Bake at 350 degrees for 1 hour. Chill in the refrigerator.

Beat the whipping cream in a mixer bowl until soft peaks form. Add the confectioners' sugar and vanilla and mix well. Store, covered, in the refrigerator until serving time.

Place a plate, cake plate or round serving tray on top of each chilled baking dish and invert. Discard the waxed paper. Cut into wedges. Drizzle each serving with about 2 tablespoons of the warm (not hot) Caramel Sauce. Top with the whipped cream.

SERVES 8

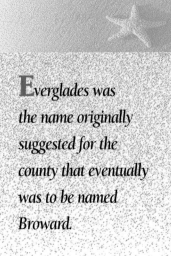

Everglades was the name originally suggested for the county that eventually was to be named Broward.

Caramel Sauce

1   cup unsalted butter
2   cups packed light brown sugar
1   cup whipping cream

Heat the butter over medium heat in a saucepan until melted. Stir in the brown sugar and whipping cream. Cook over low heat until blended, stirring constantly. Serve warm.

Note: *May be prepared in advance and stored, covered, in the refrigerator. Reheat before serving.*

Raspberry Meringues with Apricot Sauce

2   **tablespoons butter, softened**

5   **egg whites**

²/₃   **cup superfine sugar**

1   **cup prepared apricot or custard sauce**

4   **cups fresh raspberries**
       Confectioners' sugar

Coat the bottom and sides of four to six ½-cup ovenproof custard cups with the butter. Beat the egg whites in a mixer bowl until soft peaks form. Add the sugar gradually, beating constantly until stiff peaks form. Spoon the meringue into the prepared custard cups. Place the cups in a deep baking pan. Add enough boiling water to reach halfway up the sides of the cups.

Bake at 350 degrees for 10 minutes. The meringue will rise above the tops of the cups. Invert each meringue onto a dessert plate. Spoon the apricot sauce around the edge of each meringue. Top with the raspberries and sprinkle with confectioners' sugar.

SERVES 4 TO 6

Photograph for this recipe appears on page 134.

Strawberry Surprise

8   **ounces vanilla wafer crumbs**

1   **(1-pound) package confectioners' sugar**

¾   **cup butter, softened**

2   **eggs, beaten**

1   **quart fresh or frozen strawberries or raspberries**

2   **cups whipping cream**

1   **to 2 tablespoons sugar, or to taste**

Spread half of the vanilla wafer crumbs over the bottom of a 9x13-inch dish. Beat the confectioners' sugar and butter in a mixer bowl until light and fluffy. Beat in the eggs. Spread over the vanilla wafer crumbs. Slice the strawberries. Sprinkle over the top.

Beat the whipping cream and sugar in a mixer bowl until stiff peaks form. Spread over the strawberries. Sprinkle with the remaining vanilla wafer crumbs. Chill, covered, for 8 to 10 hours.

SERVES 15

Note: *To avoid raw eggs that may carry salmonella, we suggest using an equivalent amount of commercial egg substitute.*

146

Strawberry Margarita Sorbet

1½ cups water

1 cup sugar

4 pints strawberries

¼ cup tequila

2 tablespoons lime juice

2 tablespoons orange liqueur

Red tinted sugar

4 to 6 lime slices

Combine the water and sugar in a saucepan. Bring to a boil over high heat, stirring constantly. Boil until the sugar dissolves, stirring constantly. Let stand until cool.

Purée the strawberries in a blender or food processor. Strain into a bowl. Stir the tequila, lime juice and liqueur into the purée. Add to the cooled syrup mixture and mix well. Pour into an ice cream freezer container. Freeze using manufacturer's directions.

Moisten the rims of dessert goblets or nonfluted Champagne glasses with water. Spin the rims of the goblets in red tinted sugar. Spoon the sorbet into the goblets. Top each with a lime slice.

SERVES 4 TO 6

Piña Colada Ice

1 (15-ounce) can cream of coconut

1 (15-ounce) can crushed pineapple

½ cup orange juice

½ cup pineapple juice

¼ cup rum or coconut rum

½ cup shredded coconut, toasted

6 fresh pineapple slices

Process the cream of coconut, undrained crushed pineapple, orange juice and pineapple juice in a blender until smooth. Stir in the rum. Pour into an ice cream freezer container.

Freeze using manufacturer's directions. Scoop into dessert goblets. Top each serving with coconut and a pineapple slice.

SERVES 6

My Favorite Chocolate Cake

1   cup water or brewed tea

¼   cup semisweet chocolate chips

¼   cup baking cocoa

1   tablespoon vanilla instant coffee (optional)

2¼   cups packed dark brown sugar

½   cup unsalted butter, at room temperature

½   cup margarine, at room temperature

3   eggs

1   teaspoon vanilla extract

2   cups sifted cake flour

2   teaspoons baking soda

1   teaspoon baking powder

½   teaspoon salt

½   cup sour cream

½   cup vanilla yogurt

Chocolate Frosting (page 149)

Coconut Pecan Filling (page 149)

¼   cup confectioners' sugar (optional)

2   teaspoons vanilla yogurt

Grated unsweetened coconut (optional)

Blackberries and/or raspberries and sprigs of mint

Combine the water, chocolate chips, baking cocoa and coffee granules in a saucepan. Cook over low heat until smooth, stirring frequently. Let stand until cool.

Beat the brown sugar, butter and margarine in a mixer bowl until light and fluffy. Add the eggs 1 at a time, beating well after each addition. Beat in the vanilla and chocolate mixture until blended.

Sift the cake flour, baking soda, baking powder and salt into a bowl and mix well. Mix the sour cream and ½ cup yogurt in a bowl. Add the flour mixture alternately with the sour cream mixture to the chocolate mixture ⅓ at a time, beating well after each addition. Spoon into 2 greased and floured round 9-inch cake pans. Bake at 350 degrees for 25 to 30 minutes or until a wooden pick inserted in the center comes out clean. Cool in pans on a wire rack for 10 minutes. Invert onto a wire rack to cool completely.

Split each layer horizontally into halves to make 4 layers. Place 1 of the cake layers on a serving platter. Spread the top with a very thin layer of the Chocolate Frosting. Spread ¼ of the Coconut Pecan Filling over the Chocolate Frosting. Repeat this process with 2 more cake layers. Top with the remaining cake layer. Spread the top and side of the cake with a thin layer of the Chocolate Frosting; there should be Chocolate Frosting left in the bowl. Add the confectioners' sugar and 2 teaspoons yogurt to the remaining Chocolate Frosting and mix well. (This will produce a lighter brown frosting.) Spread over the top and side of the frosted cake for a marbelized effect to resemble tree bark. Spread the remaining Chocolate Pecan Filling over the top. Sprinkle with coconut. Arrange the blackberries, raspberries and sprigs of mint around the cake. Store, covered, in the refrigerator.

SERVES 12

Note: *May be prepared 1 day in advance and stored, covered, in the refrigerator.*

Coconut Pecan Filling

1   cup evaporated milk

1   cup sugar

6   tablespoons margarine

1   egg

1½ cups finely grated unsweetened coconut

½   cup finely chopped pecans

½   cup coarsely chopped pecans

Combine the evaporated milk, sugar, margarine and egg in a saucepan. Bring to a boil over medium heat, stirring constantly. Boil for 2 minutes, stirring constantly. Cool slightly. Stir in the coconut and pecans.

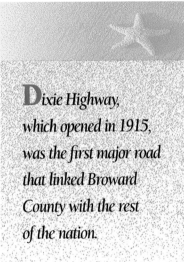

Dixie Highway, which opened in 1915, was the first major road that linked Broward County with the rest of the nation.

Chocolate Frosting

1¼ cups semisweet chocolate chips

¼   cup vanilla yogurt

½   cup sifted confectioners' sugar

Microwave the chocolate chips in a microwave-safe dish for 2 to 3 minutes or until melted. Add the yogurt and confectioners' sugar and beat until creamy.

Photograph for this recipe appears on page 134.

Chocolate Bar Cake

1   (8-ounce) milk chocolate candy bar, broken into pieces

1²/₃ cups boiling water

¹/₄   cup butter

2¹/₃ cups flour

2   cups packed light brown sugar

2   teaspoons baking soda

¹/₂   teaspoon salt

¹/₂   cup sour cream

2   eggs

1   teaspoon vanilla extract
     Chocolate Cream Cheese Frosting

Combine the candy bar, boiling water and butter in a bowl, stirring until the chocolate and butter melts.

Combine the flour, brown sugar, baking soda and salt in a mixer bowl and mix well. Add the chocolate mixture gradually, beating until blended. Add the sour cream, eggs and vanilla. Beat at medium speed for 1 minute.

Spoon the batter into 2 greased and floured 8-inch round cake pans. Bake at 350 degrees for 35 to 40 minutes or until a wooden pick inserted in the center comes out clean. Cool in pans on a wire rack for 10 minutes. Remove to a wire rack to cool completely. Spread the Chocolate Cream Cheese Frosting between the layers and over the top and side of the cake.

SERVES 8 TO 10

In 1926 the Fort Lauderdale Telephone Directory consisted of only five and one-half pages.

Chocolate Cream Cheese Frosting

9   ounces cream cheese, softened

¹/₃   cup butter or margarine, softened

5   cups confectioners' sugar

1   cup baking cocoa

5   to 7 tablespoons light cream

Beat the cream cheese and butter in a mixer bowl until light and fluffy, scraping the bowl occasionally. Add a mixture of the confectioners' sugar and baking cocoa alternately with the cream, beating well after each addition. Beat until of a spreading consistency, scraping the bowl occasionally.

Chocolate Kahlúa Cake

1	(2-layer) package pudding-recipe chocolate cake mix
2	cups sour cream
4	eggs
¾	cup vegetable oil
½	cup Kahlúa
1	cup chocolate chips

Combine the cake mix, sour cream and eggs in a bowl and mix well. Stir in the oil and Kahlúa. Fold in the chocolate chips. Spoon into a greased and floured bundt pan.

Bake at 350 degrees for 55 to 60 minutes or until the cake tests done. Cool in pan on a wire rack for 10 minutes. Remove to a wire rack to cool completely.

SERVES 10 TO 12

Note: *Serve with or decorate with a mixture of whipped cream, confectioners' sugar and Kahlúa. Garnish with fresh raspberries.*

White Butter-Frosted Cake

1	cup boiling water
⅔	cup baking cocoa
2	cups sugar
½	cup butter
2	eggs, lightly beaten
2½	cups flour
1	teaspoon baking soda
1	cup buttermilk
	White Butter Frosting

Mix the boiling water and baking cocoa in a bowl. Beat the sugar and butter in a mixer bowl until light and fluffy. Add the baking cocoa mixture and mix well. Beat in the eggs until blended. Add a mixture of sifted flour and baking soda and mix well. Add the buttermilk gradually, beating constantly until smooth. Spoon into 2 greased and floured round 8- or 9-inch cake pans.

Bake at 350 degrees for 25 to 30 minutes or until the layers test done. Cool in pans for 10 minutes. Invert onto a wire rack to cool completely. Spread the White Butter Frosting between the layers and over the top and side of the cake.

SERVES 12

White Butter Frosting

2	cups sugar
½	cup milk
½	cup butter
1	tablespoon corn syrup

Combine the sugar, milk, butter and corn syrup in a heavy saucepan. Bring to a boil, stirring occasionally. Boil to 250 to 268 degrees on a candy thermometer, hard-ball stage. Remove from heat. Cool for 10 to 15 minutes. Beat until thickened. Spread over the cake immediately.

151

Upside-Down Pineapple Cake

¼ **cup unsalted butter**

½ **cup packed light brown sugar**

8 **fresh or canned pineapple slices, patted dry**

6 **fresh or canned pineapple slices, patted dry, cut into halves**

20 **pitted sweet cherries**

¼ **cup pecan halves**

¼ **cup sour cream**

3 **egg yolks**

1 **teaspoon vanilla extract**

1½ **cups sifted flour**

¾ **cup sugar**

¾ **teaspoon baking powder**

¼ **teaspoon each baking soda and salt**

9 **tablespoons unsalted butter, softened**

¼ **cup sour cream**

Heat ¼ cup butter in a 10-inch cast-iron skillet over medium heat until melted. Add the brown sugar, stirring until blended. Remove from heat. Arrange 1 whole pineapple slice in the center of the skillet and 7 whole slices surrounding it. Arrange the pineapple halves cut edges down around the outer edge of the skillet. Place 8 of the the cherries in the center of the pineapple slices. Arrange the remaining cherries in the pineapple halves. Arrange the pecan halves in any vacant spaces.

Mix ¼ cup sour cream, egg yolks and vanilla in a bowl. Combine the flour, sugar, baking powder, baking soda and salt in a mixer bowl and mix well. Add 9 tablespoons butter and ¼ cup sour cream. Beat at low speed just until moistened, scraping the bowl occasionally. Beat at high speed for 2 minutes. Add the egg yolk mixture gradually and mix well. Spoon into the fruit-lined skillet.

Bake at 350 degrees for 40 to 50 minutes. Run a knife around the outer edge of the skillet. Invert onto a serving platter immediately.

SERVES 8 TO 10

Photograph for this recipe appears on page 134.

Fort Lauderdale's first true tourist hotel was called The Broward Hotel on Andrews Avenue. The first person registered there was movie producer D. W. Griffith in 1919.

Bev's Brownies

8	ounces unsweetened chocolate
1	cup butter
1	(16-ounce) package dark brown sugar
1/2	cup sugar
5	eggs
2	teaspoons vanilla extract
1/4	teaspoon salt
1 1/4	cups flour
2	cups semisweet or double chocolate chips
8	ounces chopped pecans or macadamia nuts

Heat the chocolate and butter in a double boiler over simmering water until blended, stirring occasionally. Cool to lukewarm, stirring occasionally. Beat the brown sugar, sugar, eggs, vanilla and salt in a mixer bowl until creamy, scraping the bowl occasionally. Add the chocolate mixture.

Beat for 2 to 3 minutes or until blended. Add the flour. Beat just until mixed. Fold in the chocolate chips and pecans. Spoon the batter into a buttered and floured 10x15-inch baking pan. Bake at 350 degrees for 45 minutes; the brownies will be slightly undercooked. Chill, covered, for 8 to 10 hours. Cut into squares.

MAKES 40 BROWNIES

Hazelnut Butter Cookies

1	(11-ounce) jar roasted hazelnut butter (about 1 cup)
1/2	cup butter, softened
1	cup packed dark brown sugar
1	cup sugar
3	eggs
2	teaspoons vanilla extract
1 1/2	teaspoons baking soda
1/2	teaspoon salt
8	ounces hazelnuts, skins removed, finely chopped
2	cups whole wheat pastry flour or all-purpose flour
1/2	cup raspberry preserves

Beat the hazelnut butter and butter in a mixer bowl at high speed until creamy, scraping the bowl occasionally. Add the brown sugar, sugar, eggs, vanilla, baking soda and salt and beat until blended. Stir in the hazelnuts. Add the whole wheat pastry flour, stirring just until moistened.

Shape the dough into 1-inch balls. Arrange 3 inches apart on a buttered cookie sheet. Flatten with a teaspoon and make a shallow indentation in the middle of each cookie. Bake at 350 degrees for 8 minutes. Spoon a teaspoon of the preserves into each indentation. Bake for 2 to 3 minutes longer. Cool on cookie sheet for 2 minutes. Remove to a wire rack to cool completely.

MAKES 2 DOZEN COOKIES

Grand Marnier Biscotti

¹/₃	cup raisins
¹/₄	cup Grand Marnier
2¹/₄	cups flour
³/₄	cup sugar
³/₄	teaspoon baking soda
¹/₄	teaspoon salt
¹/₂	cup chopped almonds or walnuts
¹/₂	cup candied cherries (optional)
1	tablespoon grated orange zest
¹/₃	cup orange juice
¹/₄	cup honey
1	teaspoon vanilla extract

Soak the raisins in the Grand Marnier in a bowl for 30 minutes. Mix the flour, sugar, baking soda and salt in a bowl. Stir in the almonds, cherries and orange zest.

Combine the orange juice, honey and vanilla in a bowl and mix well. Drain the raisins, reserving the Grand Marnier. Stir the reserved Grand Marnier into the orange juice mixture. Mix the raisins into the flour mixture. Stir the orange juice mixture into the flour mixture. Knead for several minutes or until smooth.

Divide the dough into 2 equal portions. Roll each portion into a ¹/₂-inch-thick rectangle on a lightly floured surface. Arrange the rectangles on a greased cookie sheet. Bake for 20 minutes. Let stand until cool. Cut each rectangle diagonally into slices with a serrated knife.

Arrange the slices on a cookie sheet. Bake at 300 degrees for 10 minutes; turn over the slices. Bake for 5 minutes longer. Remove to a wire rack to cool.

MAKES 2 DOZEN BISCOTTI

Note: *For variety, substitute dried cranberries for the raisins, whole wheat pastry flour for the flour, raw or light brown sugar for the white sugar, chopped pecans for the walnuts and chopped dried apricots for the candied cherries. Soak all dried fruit in the Grand Marnier.*

Chocolate Toffee Bars

2⅓ cups flour

⅔ cup packed brown sugar

¾ cup butter or margarine

1 egg, lightly beaten

2 cups semisweet chocolate chips

1 cup coarsely chopped nuts (optional)

1 (14-ounce) can sweetened condensed milk

1 (10-ounce) package toffee bits

Combine the flour and brown sugar in a bowl and mix well. Cut in the butter until crumbly. Add the egg and mix well. Stir in 1½ cups of the chocolate chips and nuts. Reserve 1½ cups of the crumb mixture.

Press the remaining crumb mixture over the bottom of a greased 9x13-inch baking pan. Bake at 350 degrees for 10 minutes. Pour the condensed milk over the baked layer. Sprinkle with the toffee bits and reserved crumb mixture. Top with the remaining ½ cup chocolate chips.

Bake for 22 to 25 minutes longer or until the edges pull from the sides of the pan. Cool in pan on a wire rack. Cut into bars.

MAKES 2 DOZEN BARS

Note: *May use low-fat or fat-free sweetened condensed milk.*

Crunchy Coconut Sandies

1½ cups plus 2½ tablespoons butter, softened

1½ cups sugar

3⅓ cups flour

¼ teaspoon salt

¾ cup Grape-Nuts cereal

½ cup shredded coconut

1 teaspoon vanilla extract

½ teaspoon coconut extract

Beat the butter and sugar in a mixer bowl until creamy, scraping the bowl occasionally. Add the flour and salt, beating until blended. Mix in the cereal, coconut and flavorings.

Shape the dough into 1-inch balls. Arrange on an ungreased cookie sheet. Bake at 375 degrees for 10 minutes or until golden brown. Cool on cookie sheet for 2 minutes. Remove to a wire rack to cool completely.

MAKES 3 DOZEN COOKIES

Crème de Menthe Brownies

½ cup margarine

2 ounces unsweetened chocolate

1 cup sugar

½ cup flour

2 eggs, lightly beaten

½ teaspoon vanilla extract

½ to 1 cup chopped pecans

2 cups confectioners' sugar

½ cup margarine, softened

3 tablespoons crème de menthe

2 tablespoons vanilla instant pudding mix

1 package chocolate fudge frosting mix

Confectioners' sugar to taste

Combine ½ cup margarine and chocolate in a saucepan. Heat just until blended, stirring frequently. Remove from heat. Add the sugar, flour, eggs and vanilla, stirring until blended. Stir in the pecans. Spoon into a 10x10-inch baking pan. Bake at 400 degrees for 15 to 20 minutes or until the edges pull from the sides of the pan. Let stand for 2 hours.

Beat 2 cups confectioners' sugar, ½ cup margarine, crème de menthe and pudding mix in a mixer bowl until creamy, scraping the bowl occasionally. Spread over the baked layer.

Prepare the frosting mix using package directions and adding the desired amount of confectioners' sugar to yield a richer flavor. Spread over the crème de menthe layer. Chill, covered, for 3 hours.

MAKES 2 TO 3 DOZEN BROWNIES

Sunflower Seed Cookies

3 cups quick-cooking oats

1½ cups flour

1 teaspoon baking soda

½ teaspoon salt

1 cup margarine

1 cup packed light brown sugar

1 cup sugar

2 extra-large eggs

1 teaspoon vanilla extract

1 cup sunflower seed kernels

Mix the oats, flour, baking soda and salt in a bowl. Beat the margarine, brown sugar, sugar, eggs and vanilla in a mixer bowl until creamy, scraping the bowl occasionally. Add the oats mixture gradually and mix well. Stir in the sunflower seed kernels.

Drop by teaspoonfuls onto an ungreased cookie sheet. Bake at 350 degrees for 10 minutes. Cool on cookie sheet for 2 minutes. Remove to a wire rack to cool completely.

MAKES 3 TO 4 DOZEN COOKIES

Lemon Chess Pie

4	eggs
2	cups sugar
¼	cup butter, softened
¼	teaspoon salt
1	tablespoon flour
1	tablespoon cornmeal
¼	cup milk
½	to ¾ cup lemon juice
	Grated peel of 2 or 3 lemons
1	unbaked (9-inch) pie shell

Beat the eggs in a mixer bowl until blended. Add the sugar, butter, salt, flour, cornmeal, milk, lemon juice and lemon peel in the order listed, beating well after each addition. Spoon into the pie shell. (Don't worry if the mixture looks curdled.)

Bake at 425 degrees for 10 minutes. Reduce the oven temperature to 225 degrees. Bake for 40 minutes longer.

SERVES 6

Note: *Cover the edge of the pastry with foil to prevent overbrowning. Remove the foil 20 minutes before the end of the baking process.*

Key Lime Tarts

2	cups unbleached flour
¼	cup finely chopped walnuts
½	cup butter or margarine, softened
½	cup sugar
3	egg yolks, lightly beaten
1	teaspoon vanilla extract
3	cups sweetened condensed milk
⅓	cup Key lime juice
	Sweetened whipped cream
1	or 2 Key limes, thinly sliced

Mix the flour and walnuts in a bowl. Add the butter, sugar, egg yolks and vanilla, mixing with a fork until the mixture forms a ball. (Use a food processor if desired.) Chill, covered, for 2 to 10 hours.

Roll the pastry on a lightly floured surface. Fit the pastry into individual tart pans; prick sides and bottoms with a fork. Bake at 325 degrees for 10 to 20 minutes or until golden brown. Let stand until cool.

Mix the condensed milk and Key lime juice in a bowl. Spoon into the cooled tart shells. Chill, covered, until serving time. Top each tart with sweetened whipped cream and lime slices just before serving.

MAKES 6 TO 8 TARTS

Note: *To make this dessert even quicker to prepare, spoon the filling into a commercially prepared graham cracker crust or 9- or 10-inch baked pie shell.*

Photograph for this recipe appears on page 134.

WAVE REVIEWS

THE BEST OF

SUNNY SIDE UP

Sponsored by

JUNIOR LEAGUE OF GREATER
FORT LAUDERDALE SUSTAINERS

Bagna Cauda

3	cups whipping cream
2	tablespoons unsalted butter
6	anchovies, finely chopped
1/8	teaspoon white pepper
2	tablespoons finely chopped garlic, or to taste
2	tablespoons flour
	Assorted fresh vegetables

Heat the whipping cream in a saucepan over medium heat. Combine the butter, anchovies, white pepper and garlic in a saucepan. Simmer over low heat until of the consistency of a thick paste, stirring occasionally. Stir in the flour until blended. Add the anchovy mixture to the whipping cream and mix well.

Simmer until thickened, stirring occasionally. The flavor and consistency of the dip is enhanced the longer the simmering process. Serve with assorted fresh vegetables.

SERVES 8 TO 10

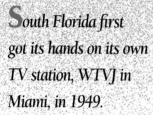

South Florida first got its hands on its own TV station, WTVJ in Miami, in 1949.

Shrimp Cheese Broil

	Melba toast rounds
1	pound small shrimp, steamed, peeled, deveined
1/2	cup mayonnaise
1/4	cup grated Parmesan cheese
2	teaspoons minced onion
	Sesame seeds

Arrange the toast rounds in a single layer on baking sheets. Top each round with a shrimp.

Combine the mayonnaise, cheese and onion in a bowl. Spoon over the shrimp. Sprinkle with sesame seeds. Broil until brown and bubbly.

MAKES 3 DOZEN

Note: *May substitute sliced marinated artichoke hearts for the shrimp. This is also delicious as a spread for an open-face sandwich on lightly toasted bread.*

OVERLEAF: *Key Lime Bars*

White Sangria

2   (1.5 liter) bottles Rhine wine

½   cup brandy

1   cup curaçao

1   (10-ounce) package frozen strawberries, thawed

1   (16-ounce) package frozen mixed fruit, sliced

2   oranges, cut into quarters

2   Key limes or 1 lime, cut into quarters

1   lemon, cut into quarters

     Sugar to taste

1   banana, sliced

1   quart club soda

Combine the wine, brandy and curaçao in a large container. Add the strawberries, mixed fruit, oranges, limes and lemon. Stir in the desired amount of sugar. Chill for 24 hours. Add the banana and club soda just before serving.

MAKES 25 SERVINGS

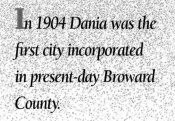

In 1904 Dania was the first city incorporated in present-day Broward County.

Yucca Blossoms

1   (6-ounce) can frozen limeade concentrate

1   limeade can vodka

1   tablespoon (heaping) shredded coconut, or powdered coconut to taste

     Cracked ice

Combine the limeade concentrate, vodka, coconut and ice in a blender container. Process until blended. Pour into large wine or whiskey sour glasses.

SERVES 4

Sustainer's Slush

1	**(12-ounce) can frozen lemonade concentrate**
4½	**cups water**
3	**cups bourbon**
3	**tablespoons frozen orange juice concentrate**

Combine the lemonade concentrate, water, bourbon and orange juice concentrate in a freezer container and mix well. Freeze until firm. Spoon into goblets.

SERVES 12 TO 14

Curried Chicken Salad

2	**cups chopped cooked chicken**
1	**(8-ounce) can pineapple chunks, drained**
8	**ounces seedless green grapes, cut into halves**
½	**cup chopped celery**
½	**cup slivered almonds, toasted**
¼	**cup sliced water chestnuts**
	Curry Dressing

Mix the chicken, pineapple, grapes, celery, almonds and water chestnuts in a bowl. Add the Curry Dressing, tossing to coat. Chill, covered, for several hours.

SERVES 4

Note: *This recipe was created for a luncheon hosted by the University of Virginia for Queen Elizabeth II.*

Curry Dressing

¾	**cup mayonnaise**
2	**teaspoons soy sauce**
2	**teaspoons lemon juice**
1	**teaspoon curry powder**

Combine the mayonnaise, soy sauce, lemon juice and curry powder in a bowl and mix well.

Cold Steak Salad

2	pounds sirloin, cut into $\frac{1}{2}$-inch pieces
$\frac{1}{2}$	cup butter
12	ounces mushrooms, sliced
1	(10-ounce) package frozen artichoke hearts, cooked, drained, cooled
1	cup chopped celery
2	cups small cherry tomatoes
2	tablespoons chopped fresh chives
2	tablespoons chopped fresh parsley
2	cups Dijon Dressing
	Lettuce leaves

Sauté the beef in $\frac{1}{4}$ cup of the butter in a skillet until medium-rare. Transfer the beef to a colander to drain. Let stand until cool. Sauté the mushrooms in the remaining $\frac{1}{4}$ cup butter in a skillet; drain. Let stand until cool.

Combine the beef, mushrooms, artichokes, celery, cherry tomatoes, chives and parsley in a bowl and mix gently. Add the Dijon dressing, tossing to coat. Marinate, covered, in the refrigerator for 8 to 10 hours, stirring occasionally. Spoon onto lettuce-lined salad plates.

SERVES 6

The most costly war before the Vietnam War was not World War I or II but the Seminole War, which cost $40 million dollars. Technically it's not over as a peace treaty was never signed.

Dijon Dressing

$2\frac{1}{4}$	cups vegetable oil
$\frac{3}{4}$	cup wine vinegar
$\frac{1}{3}$	cup chopped fresh parsley
6	shallots, finely chopped
2	teaspoons Dijon mustard
$1\frac{1}{2}$	teaspoons dried dillweed, or $\frac{1}{3}$ cup chopped fresh dillweed
$\frac{1}{8}$	teaspoon Tabasco sauce
	Salt and pepper to taste

Combine the oil, wine vinegar, parsley, shallots, Dijon mustard, dillweed, Tabasco sauce, salt and pepper in a jar with a tightfitting lid. Cover the jar and shake to mix. Store in the refrigerator.

Frito Salad

1	**head iceberg lettuce, torn**
2	**tomatoes, chopped**
6	**scallions with tops, chopped**
1	**(15-ounce) can kidney beans, drained, rinsed**
2	**cups shredded Cheddar cheese**
1	**(11-ounce) package Fritos, crushed**
1	**(8-ounce) bottle Catalina salad dressing**

Toss the lettuce, tomatoes, scallions, beans and cheese in a bowl. (May be prepared in advance to this point and stored, covered, in the refrigerator until just before serving.) Add the Fritos and salad dressing just before serving and mix well.

SERVES 12

Racquet Club Pineapple Salad

1	**head romaine, torn**
1	**bunch watercress, trimmed**
2	**scallions, chopped**
1	**(14-ounce) can pineapple tidbits, drained**
1	**avocado, chopped**
2	**tomatoes, peeled, chopped**
3	**hard-cooked eggs, chopped**
8	**slices crisp-fried bacon, crumbled**
3	**ounces bleu cheese, crumbled**
1/2	**cup vegetable oil**
3	**tablespoons garlic-flavor wine vinegar**
1 1/2	**teaspoons seasoned salt**
	Freshly ground pepper to taste

Toss the romaine, watercress and scallions in a salad bowl. Arrange the pineapple, avocado, tomatoes, eggs and bacon over the greens. Sprinkle with the bleu cheese.

Whisk the oil, wine vinegar, seasoned salt and pepper in a bowl. Drizzle over the salad and toss lightly just before serving.

SERVES 6

Note: *May substitute ham, chicken or shrimp for the bacon.*

Splendid Salad

1/3   **cup wine vinegar**

1   **tablespoon Greek seasoning**

1 1/2   **teaspoons sugar**

1   **teaspoon salt**

1   **teaspoon brown mustard**

1/2   **cup mayonnaise**

1/3   **cup each olive oil and safflower oil**

4   **or 5 heads Bibb lettuce, torn**

1   **cup shredded coconut, toasted**

1   **cup slivered almonds, toasted**

1   **(11-ounce) can mandarin oranges**

    Cherry tomatoes

1   **pound shrimp, steamed, peeled**

    Freshly ground pepper to taste

Combine the wine vinegar, Greek seasoning, sugar, salt and brown mustard in a food processor. Process for 30 seconds. Add the mayonnaise, olive oil and safflower oil gradually, processing constantly until blended. Chill, covered, for 1 hour before serving.

Toss the lettuce, coconut, almonds, drained mandarin oranges, cherry tomatoes and shrimp in a large salad bowl. Add the dressing and mix well. Sprinkle with pepper just before serving.

SERVES 4 TO 6

Father's Day Steak

1/2   **cup each sherry and soy sauce**

1/4   **cup vegetable oil**

1/4   **cup lemon juice**

2   **tablespoons brown sugar**

1/2   **teaspoon ginger**

1/8   **teaspoon hot sauce**

1   **clove of garlic, minced**

1   **(3- to 4-pound) London broil or top round steak**

4   **teaspoons cornstarch**

8   **ounces mushrooms, sliced**

1/4   **cup sliced scallions**

Combine the sherry, soy sauce, oil, lemon juice, brown sugar, ginger, hot sauce and garlic in a saucepan and mix well. Cook for 10 minutes, stirring occasionally. Let stand until cool.

Place the steak in a sealable plastic bag. Pour the sherry mixture over the steak; seal tightly. Marinate in the refrigerator for 24 hours, turning occasionally. Drain, reserving the marinade.

Place the steak on a broiler rack. Broil 4 to 5 inches from the heat source for 25 to 40 minutes for rare to medium, turning and brushing with the reserved marinade occasionally. Transfer the steak to a serving platter. Cut diagonally across the grain into thin slices.

Combine the cornstarch with a small amount of water in a saucepan. Stir in the remaining reserved marinade. Bring to a boil; reduce heat. Stir in the mushrooms and scallions. Cook until thickened or until of a sauce consistency, stirring constantly. May add additional water to reach desired consistency. Serve with the steak.

SERVES 6 TO 8

Breast of Chicken Alexis

12	boneless skinless chicken breast halves
	Salt to taste
1/4	cup chopped onion
1/2	cup butter
2	cups dry stuffing mix
1	cup grated carrots
1/2	cup chopped dates
1/3	cup sliced almonds
1/2	teaspoon rosemary
	Melted butter
1	orange, sliced
	Orange Date Sauce
1 1/4	cups orange juice
1 1/2	teaspoons flour
1/2	teaspoon salt
1/2	cup chopped dates

Pound the chicken between sheets of waxed paper until flattened. Sprinkle with salt.

Sauté the onion in 1/2 cup butter in a skillet until tender. Add the stuffing, carrots, dates, almonds and rosemary and toss to mix. Spoon some of the stuffing mixture in the center of each chicken breast. Roll to enclose the filling; secure with wooden picks. Arrange the chicken seam side down in a nonstick baking pan. Brush with melted butter.

Bake at 300 degrees for 1 1/2 hours, basting with the pan drippings frequently. Transfer the chicken to a heated platter with a slotted spoon, reserving the pan drippings. Top each chicken breast with orange slices and drizzle with some of the Orange Date Sauce. Serve with the remaining Orange Date Sauce.

SERVES 12

Orange Date Sauce

Combine 1/4 cup of the orange juice and flour in a saucepan and mix well. Stir in the reserved pan drippings, remaining 1 cup orange juice and salt. Cook until thickened, stirring constantly. Fold in the dates.

Spinach Danielle

2	(10-ounce) packages frozen spinach
1	cup sour cream
1	envelope onion soup mix
1/2	cup butter or margarine
1 1/2	cups dry stuffing mix

Cook the spinach using package directions; drain. Squeeze any remaining moisture from the spinach. Combine the sour cream and soup mix in a bowl and mix well. Add the spinach and mix well.

Heat the butter in a saucepan until melted. Stir in the stuffing. Pat half the stuffing mixture over the bottom of a 1 1/2-quart baking dish. Spread with the spinach mixture. Top with the remaining stuffing mixture. Bake at 325 degrees for 30 minutes.

SERVES 6

Southern Cheese Grits

6	cups water
1	teaspoon salt
1½	cups grits
8	to 12 ounces Cheddar cheese, shredded
¾	cup butter
1	teaspoon salt
1	drop of Tabasco sauce
1	medium onion, chopped (optional)
3	eggs, beaten
1	teaspoon paprika

Bring the water and 1 teaspoon salt to a boil in a saucepan. Stir in the grits. Cook for 20 minutes, stirring occasionally. Stir in the cheese, butter, 1 teaspoon salt and Tabasco sauce. Fold in the onion and beaten eggs.

Spoon the grits mixture into a buttered 1½-quart baking dish. Sprinkle with the paprika. Bake at 250 degrees for 1 hour.

SERVES 8 TO 10

Note: *Serve as a substitute for potatoes.*

Champagne Snapper

4	snapper fillets
1	teaspoon salt
½	teaspoon pepper
1	cup Champagne or dry white wine
2	tablespoons butter
1	bay leaf
1	tablespoon chopped onion
1	tablespoon finely chopped celery with leaves
2	teaspoons finely chopped fresh parsley
2	tablespoons cream
⅓	cup sliced mushrooms
3	tablespoons freshly grated Parmesan cheese

Sprinkle both sides of the fillets with the salt and pepper. Arrange in a single layer in a buttered 9x13-inch baking dish.

Combine the Champagne, 2 tablespoons butter, bay leaf, onion, celery and parsley in a saucepan. Bring to a boil; reduce heat. Simmer until reduced by half, stirring frequently. Discard the bay leaf. Stir in the cream. Remove from heat.

Add the mushrooms to the sauce. Pour over the fillets. Sprinkle with the cheese. Bake at 350 degrees for 25 to 30 minutes or until brown and bubbly.

SERVES 4

Note: *May substitute sole or cod for the snapper.*

Florida Orange Bread

4   cups flour
4   teaspoons baking powder
2   teaspoons salt
$\frac{1}{2}$ teaspoon baking soda
$1\frac{1}{2}$ cups sugar
$\frac{1}{3}$ cup water
$\frac{3}{4}$ cup slivered orange peel
3   tablespoons butter
$1\frac{1}{3}$ cups orange juice
3   eggs, beaten

Grease a 6x10-inch loaf pan and line with waxed paper. Sift the flour, baking powder, salt and baking soda together.

Combine the sugar and water in a saucepan. Stir in the orange peel. Cook until the sugar dissolves, stirring constantly. Remove from heat. Cool for 5 minutes. Add the butter, stirring until blended. Stir in the orange juice and eggs.

Add the dry ingredients, stirring just until moistened; batter will be lumpy. Spoon into the prepared loaf pan. Bake at 325 degrees for $1\frac{1}{4}$ hours.

MAKES 1 LOAF

Where the Boys Are was a popular movie made on Fort Lauderdale Beach in 1960, starring Connie Francis, George Hamilton, and Paula Prentiss, among others.

Carrot Cake

2   **cups sifted flour**

2½ **teaspoons cinnamon**

2   **teaspoons baking powder**

1½ **teaspoons baking soda**

1   **teaspoon salt**

2   **cups sugar**

1½ **cups vegetable oil**

4   **eggs**

2   **cups finely grated carrots**

1   **(8-ounce) can crushed pineapple, drained**

1   **(4-ounce) can flaked coconut**

⅓   **cup chopped pecans**
    Cream Cheese Frosting

Sift the flour, cinnamon, baking powder, baking soda and salt into a bowl and mix well. Stir in the sugar, oil and eggs. Add the carrots, pineapple, coconut and pecans and mix well.

Spoon the batter into 3 greased and floured 9-inch cake pans. Bake at 350 degrees for 35 to 40 minutes or until the layers test done.

Cool in the pans for 10 minutes. Invert onto wire racks to cool completely. Spread the Cream Cheese Frosting between the layers and over the top and side of the cake.

SERVES 10

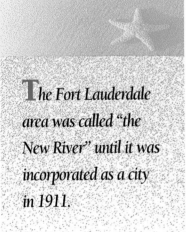

The Fort Lauderdale area was called "the New River" until it was incorporated as a city in 1911.

Cream Cheese Frosting

8   **ounces cream cheese, softened**

½   **cup butter or margarine, softened**

1¼ **teaspoons vanilla extract**

1   **(1-pound) package confectioners' sugar**

Beat the cream cheese, butter and vanilla in a mixer bowl until light and fluffy. Add the confectioners' sugar. Beat until of a spreading consistency, adding a small amount of milk if needed for the desired consistency.

Key Lime Bars

1   cup flour
¼   cup confectioners' sugar
½   cup butter, softened
2   eggs, lightly beaten
1   cup sugar
2   tablespoons flour
⅓   cup Key lime juice
2   tablespoons sifted confectioners' sugar

Combine 1 cup flour and ¼ cup confectioners' sugar in a bowl and mix well. Add the butter, stirring or processing in a food processor until the mixture forms a ball. Pat the dough with lightly floured fingers over the bottom of a greased 8x8-inch baking pan. Bake at 350 degrees for 15 to 20 minutes.

Mix the eggs and sugar in a bowl. Stir in 2 tablespoons flour. Add the Key lime juice and mix well. Spread over the warm baked layer. Bake for 20 to 25 minutes. Cool in the pan on a wire rack. Sprinkle with 2 tablespoons sifted confectioners' sugar. Cut into bars.

MAKES 2 DOZEN BARS

Note: *If Key lime juice is not available, use regular lime juice.*

Photograph for this recipe appears on page 158.

The Native American Indians were not allowed alcohol at Frank Stranahan's Trading Post, so they'd canoe to other settlements to be served. Ivy Stranahan would request at least one remain sober and be the "designated canoer."

Oatmeal Cookies

1½   cups raisins
1½   cups sifted flour
1   teaspoon each cinnamon, salt and baking soda
1   cup shortening
1   cup each packed brown sugar and sugar
2   eggs
1   teaspoon vanilla extract
3   cups rolled oats

Plump the raisins in hot water to cover in a bowl; drain. Sift the flour, cinnamon, salt and baking soda together.

Beat the shortening, brown sugar and sugar in a bowl until creamy, scraping the bowl occasionally. Add the eggs and vanilla. Beat until blended. Add the flour mixture and beat until smooth. Stir in the raisins and oats. Drop by teaspoonfuls onto an ungreased cookie sheet. Bake at 325 degrees for 6 to 8 minutes. Cool on the cookie sheet for 2 minutes. Remove to a wire rack to cool completely.

MAKES 8 DOZEN COOKIES

170

Amaretto Coconut Cream Pie

1¼ cups shredded coconut
2 envelopes unflavored gelatin
⅓ cup cold water
1 cup graham cracker crumbs
¼ cup sugar
¼ cup melted butter
1 cup sugar
4 eggs
½ cup amaretto
⅛ teaspoon almond extract
4 cups whipping cream, whipped
12 fresh strawberries

Spread the coconut on a baking sheet. Toast at 350 degrees for 15 minutes or until golden brown, stirring frequently. Sprinkle the gelatin over the cold water in an ovenproof bowl. Let stand for 5 minutes. Set the bowl in a saucepan filled with hot water. Heat over low heat until the gelatin dissolves, stirring frequently. Grease the bottom of a 10-inch springform pan. Mix the graham cracker crumbs, ¼ cup sugar and butter in a bowl. Press the crumb mixture over the bottom of the prepared pan.

Beat 1 cup sugar and eggs in a mixer bowl until fluffy. Fold in the gelatin mixture, amaretto and flavoring. Let stand until slightly thickened. Reserve a small amount of the coconut for the top. Fold the remaining coconut and whipped cream into the egg mixture. Spoon into the prepared pan. Chill, covered, until set. Sprinkle with the reserved coconut and top with the strawberries just before serving.

SERVES 12

Note: *To avoid raw eggs that may carry salmonella, we suggest using an equivalent amount of commercial egg substitute.*

Margarita Pie

1½ cups crushed pretzels
¼ cup sugar
½ cup melted butter
1 (14-ounce) can sweetened condensed milk
⅓ cup fresh lime juice
2 tablespoons tequila
2 tablespoons Triple Sec
1 or 2 drops of green food coloring
1 cup whipping cream, whipped
   Lime slices

Mix the pretzels and sugar in a bowl. Add the butter, stirring until crumbly. Press the crumb mixture over the bottom and up the side of a 9-inch buttered pie plate. Chill in the refrigerator.

Combine the condensed milk, lime juice, tequila and Triple Sec in a bowl and mix well. Stir in the food coloring. Fold in the whipped cream. Spoon into the prepared pie plate.

Freeze, covered, for 3 to 4 hours or until firm. Top each serving with a lime slice.

SERVES 8 TO 10

Note: *May be stored in the freezer for several days.*

EVERYTHING UNDER THE SUN

KIDS, GIFTS, ETC.

Sponsored by

ANN WALDROP GRIFFIN

Caramel Corn

2   cups packed brown sugar
1   cup butter
1/2 cup light corn syrup
1   teaspoon salt
1   teaspoon baking soda
6   quarts popcorn, popped
   Peanuts (optional)

Heat the brown sugar, butter and corn syrup in a saucepan until blended, stirring frequently. Stir in the salt. Bring to a boil, stirring constantly. Boil for 5 minutes. Remove from heat. Add the baking soda, stirring until foamy. Combine the popcorn and peanuts in a buttered disposable pan. Pour the brown sugar mixture over the popcorn mixture and mix well.

Bake at 200 degrees for 1 hour, stirring every 15 minutes. Let stand until cool. Store in an airtight container.

SERVES 10

Note: *Fill cellophane bags with the Caramel Corn and tie with festive ribbon for great holiday gifts.*

Fort Lauderdale was the first land to be discovered and the last Florida land to be settled.

Taco Cheese Animal Crackers

1½ cups shredded taco-flavor Cheddar cheese
1   cup flour
1/2 cup butter or margarine, softened
   Paprika to taste

Combine the cheese, flour and butter in a food processor container fitted with a steel blade. Process until the mixture forms a ball, scraping the side of the bowl once. Chill, wrapped in plastic wrap, for 30 minutes.

Roll the dough ½ inch thick on a lightly floured surface. Cut with animal cookie cutters. Arrange on a baking sheet. Sprinkle with paprika. Bake at 375 degrees for 10 to 12 minutes or until light brown. Cool on the baking sheet for 2 minutes. Remove to a wire rack to cool completely.

MAKES 3 DOZEN CRACKERS

OVERLEAF: *Sand Pail Pudding*

174

Cheese Nip Chicken

Cheese crackers or Goldfish
crackers

4   boneless skinless chicken breast
halves

2   cups sour cream

1/2 cup melted butter

Fill a sealable plastic sandwich bag with cheese crackers and seal. Crush the crackers in the bag. Coat the chicken with the sour cream. Place the chicken and cracker crumbs in a large sealable plastic bag and shake to coat Arrange the chicken in a single layer in a greased 9x13-inch baking dish. Drizzle with the butter. Bake at 350 degrees for 30 minutes or until cooked through.

SERVES 4

"Cop-Out" Pizza Pretendo

2   pounds mild or hot sausage

2   (14-ounce) jars pizza sauce

16 ounces egg noodles, cooked,
drained

3   cups (or more) shredded
mozzarella cheese

2   (3-ounce) packages sliced
pepperoni

1/4 cup grated Parmesan cheese

Brown the sausage in a skillet, stirring until crumbly; drain. Combine the sausage, pizza sauce and noodles in a bowl and mix well.

Layer the sausage mixture and mozzarella cheese alternately in a baking pan until all of the ingredients are used. Arrange the pepperoni over the top. Sprinkle with the Parmesan cheese. Bake at 350 degrees for 30 minutes.

SERVES 6

Cupcakes in a Cone

2	cups flour
2	teaspoons baking powder
1	teaspoon baking soda
1	teaspoon cinnamon
1	teaspoon salt
2	cups sugar
1¼	cups vegetable oil
4	eggs
3	cups grated carrots
1	(18-count) package ice cream cones with flat bottoms
	Cream Cheese Frosting
	Jelly beans or candy corn

Line 18 muffin cups with parchment paper. Sift the flour, baking powder, baking soda, cinnamon and salt into a bowl and mix well.

Mix the sugar and oil in a bowl. Add half the flour mixture and mix well. Add the remaining flour mixture alternately with the eggs 1 at a time, mixing well after each addition. Stir in the carrots. Spoon the batter into the cones, filling ¾ full. Place the cones in the prepared muffin cups.

Bake at 350 degrees for 25 minutes or until a wooden pick inserted in the center of the cupcakes comes out clean. Remove the cones to a wire rack to cool. Spread with the Cream Cheese Frosting. Top with jelly beans or candy corn.

MAKES 18 CUPCAKES

Early South Florida settlers used to tie kerosene rags around the bottom of each table leg to keep the ants from crawling up to the food.

Cream Cheese Frosting

8	ounces cream cheese, softened
½	cup butter, softened
1	teaspoon vanilla extract
1	(1-pound) package confectioners' sugar

Beat the cream cheese, butter and vanilla in a mixer bowl until light and fluffy. Add the confectioners' sugar gradually, beating until of a spreading consistency and scraping the bowl occasionally.

Sand Pail Pudding

2 or 3 (6-ounce) packages vanilla instant pudding mix

1 package vanilla wafers

1½ to 2 cups confectioners' sugar

1 cup peanut butter

1 medium sand pail, or 6 to 8 (3-ounce) sand pails and shovels

Gummy candies

Prepare the pudding mix using package directions. Chill, covered, in the refrigerator. Process the vanilla wafers in a food processor until crushed. Mix the confectioners' sugar and peanut butter in a bowl until crumbly, adding additional confectioners' sugar as needed for the desired consistency.

Layer the peanut butter mixture and pudding mixture ½ at a time in the sand pail or sand pails. Top with the vanilla wafer crumbs. Decorate with gummy candies. Serve with the shovels.

SERVES 6 TO 8

Photograph for this recipe appears on page 172.

Smiley Cake

1 cup stick butter, softened

3 cups pancake batter

Maple syrup, heated

Pat the butter sticks between sheets of waxed paper to ½-inch thickness. Chill until firm. Cut shapes (stars, circles, half-moons, hearts or just use your imagination) from the butter with miniature cookie cutters or with a knife, reserving the remnants to cook the pancakes. Arrange the butter shapes between sheets of waxed paper. Store in the refrigerator in an airtight container.

Heat the butter remnants in a skillet until melted. Create a smiley face by dropping 1 teaspoon of the batter at a time into the skillet for the eyes and drizzling another teaspoon of the batter in the skillet for a smile. Do not spread the smile out too far because this will determine the size of the pancake. Pour the batter over the eyes and mouth to form the whole pancake. Cook for 1½ to 2 minutes or until the bubbles burst; turn over the pancake. When you turn the pancake, you will see the smiley face is darker than the rest of the pancake. Cook for 1 to 2 minutes or until golden brown. Remove to an ovenproof platter. Keep warm in a 200-degree oven. Serve buffet-style with the butter shapes and maple syrup.

SERVES 4

Frozen Fudge Pops

1 **(4-ounce) package chocolate pudding and pie filling mix**

3 **cups milk**

¼ **cup sugar**

½ **cup whipping cream, whipped**

Whisk the pudding mix, milk and sugar in a saucepan. Bring to a boil. Cook for 2 minutes, stirring constantly. Cool for 30 minutes. Fold in the whipped cream.

Spoon the pudding mixture into individual popsicle molds. Freeze for 3 to 4 hours or until firm.

MAKES 12 POPSICLES

Note: *Add sliced strawberries or bananas with the whipped cream for variety.*

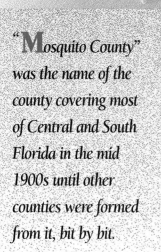

"Mosquito County" was the name of the county covering most of Central and South Florida in the mid 1900s until other counties were formed from it, bit by bit.

Yogurt Popsicles

2 **cups plain yogurt**

1 **(6-ounce) can frozen grape juice concentrate**

2 **teaspoons vanilla or almond extract**

Combine the yogurt, grape juice concentrate and vanilla in a bowl and mix well. Spoon into small paper cups. Cover with plastic wrap and insert a plastic spoon or wooden popsicle stick through the plastic. Freeze until firm. May freeze in popsicle molds.

MAKES 6 TO 8 POPSICLES

Rock-and-Roll Ice Cream

2	**cups half-and-half**
½	**cup sugar**
1	**teaspoon vanilla extract**
1	**(1-pound) empty coffee can with lid**
6	**to 7 cups crushed ice**
1	**(3-pound) empty coffee can with lid**
¾	**cup rock salt**

Mix the half-and-half, sugar and vanilla in a bowl. Pour into the 1-pound coffee can and seal tightly with the lid. Spread a thin layer of the crushed ice over the bottom of the 3-pound coffee can. Sprinkle with 1 tablespoon of the rock salt. Place the smaller coffee can right side up in the larger coffee can. Pack the area between the cans with the remaining crushed ice and remaining rock salt, using about 2 tablespoons rock salt per cup of ice. Seal tightly with the lid. Roll the can back and forth across the counter or floor, protected with a towel, for 10 to 15 minutes. Remove the smaller can and lid carefully. Scrape down the sides of the can and stir the ice cream. Check for the desired consistency. Repack with ice and salt and roll for several more minutes for a firmer consistency if needed.

SERVES 5

Gobblers

1	**(16-ounce) package chocolate sandwich cookies**
¼	**cup red hot cinnamon candies**
1¼	**cups malted milk balls**
1	**(16-ounce) container chocolate frosting**
1	**(10-ounce) package candy corn**

Separate the cookies, leaving the cream filling intact on 1 side. Attach a red hot candy to each malted milk ball with a small amount of the chocolate frosting to make the turkey head and body. Attach each turkey body with some of the chocolate frosting to the center of each cookie half with the cream filling. This forms the base for the cookie. Spread the inside of the remaining cookie halves without the cream filling with some of the remaining chocolate frosting. Arrange the candy corn with points facing outward along the outer edge of the frosting to form the tail. Attach a tail perpendicular to each turkey body with the remaining frosting. Store, covered, in the refrigerator until just before serving.

MAKES 42 GOBBLERS

Note: *This is a great project for the children while you are preparing Thanksgiving dinner!*

Papier-Mâché Mask

1   cup water
1   cup flour
     Newspapers or paper bags, torn
     into strips

Combine the water and flour in a saucepan. Cook over medium heat until bubbly, stirring constantly. Remove from heat. Stir until thickened. (The mixture will continue to thicken as it cools.)

Form mask by using a bowl, balloon or plate as a mold. Invert the desired bowl on a hard surface covered with additional newspapers or towels. Coat the outside of the bowl with petroleum jelly and cover with plastic wrap. Saturate the newspaper strips in the papier-mâché mixture. Arrange the strips over the plastic wrap. Let stand until dry. May also use the inside of the bowl as a smaller-size mold.

MAKES 1 MASK

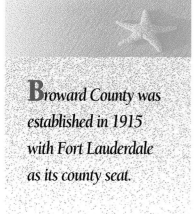

Broward County was established in 1915 with Fort Lauderdale as its county seat.

Peanut Butter Play Dough

4   cups quick-cooking oats
2   cups flour
1   cup water
1¼   cups dry milk powder
1¼   cups sifted confectioners' sugar
1   cup light corn syrup
1   cup peanut butter

Process the oats and flour in a blender for 30 seconds. Combine the oat mixture and water in a bowl and mix well. Knead briefly. Stir in the milk powder, confectioners' sugar, corn syrup and peanut butter. Knead briefly. May add additional milk powder if the dough appears too sticky.

SERVES 6 TO 8

Note: *Do not worry if your children decide to eat the play dough. It is edible!*

Acknowledgments

For their many and varied contributions in the making of *Made In The Shade*,
the Junior League of Greater Fort Lauderdale thanks…

Anne Andreae, Anne Andreae Design

Janet Carpenter

Kathleen and Jeff Denis, Denis Watercolors

Gina Goodrum

Barry Grossman and Alex Grossman, Optic Nerve

Lisa Hilowitz

Andrew Itkoff

Wendy Jackson

Cindy Mahoney

Neiman Marcus

Ann McCrory

Peter Nolan, The Digital Tree

Pier 1 Imports

Howard Plotkin

Pottery Barn

Publix

Jane Radanoff

Victoria Taylor

Jennifer Tkachyk

Dolly van Hengel, Lily Whites

Sylvia Wallace, Antiques & Country Pine

Cookbook Committees

1995-1996
Fund Development Steering Committee
Chairs

Sue Ellen Boatright

Kristin Markham

Committee Members

Paige Ashley

Stephanie Budin • *Denise Colon*

Sonali Garvin • *Julie Johnston* • *Joan Morris*

Corrine Nienstedt • *Shavawn Peterson*

1996-1997
Chairs

Stephanie Budin • *Traci Schuh*

Committee Members

Linda Reid Askinas

Jean Cabot • *Carol DeGraffenreidt*

Cynthia Economou • *Leslie Flavell*

Kim Geisland • *Ann Griffin*

Gennifer Jett

Laura Kelly • *Kim Liang* • *Kim Nava*

Connie Ordeman • *Sara Sears* • *Colleen Smalley*

Jane Smith • *Jan Timberlin* • *Christine Welch*

Beth Welker

Sustaining Advisor

Jennifer Smith

1997-1998

Chairs

Mary Lois Faulhaber

Traci Schuh

Beth Welker

Committee Members

Linda Reid Askinas

Claire Brown

Cheramie Burgess • Barbara Burke

Carol DeGraffenreidt

Lillian Aylwn Dickson

Robin Dunn • Julie Flavell

Leslie Flavell

Leah Glenewinkel

Shannon Graulich

Ann Griffin • Sherry Hannaka

Susan Hirsch • Gennifer Jett

Elizabeth Kasperovich

Kristin Markham • Jeanne McKiethen

Pam Monast

Kim Nava • Gwen Rinehart

Heather Shaw

Cathy Sheehan

Sustaining Advisor

Barbara Bookman

1998-1999

Chairs

Victoria Artel

Cathy Sheehan

Committee Members

Linda Askinas

Rachel Bailey

Claire Brown

Barbara Burke • Lisa Danyluk

Nancy Lynn Dixon

Alisa Duke • Barbara Ericksen

Bethany Fee

Leslie Flavell • Vickie Gilman

Susan Grant • Heidi Gray

Jane Greenwood

Laura Minor

Susan Molnar

Pam Monast • Barbara Newton

Alisa Oglesby

Maria Pierson • Alexandra Roumain

Sustaining Advisor

Barbara Bookman

1999-2000

Chairs

Victoria Artel

Cathy Sheehan

Committee Members

Monica Andrews

Rachel Bailey • Barbara Burke

Molly Cataldo • Karen Ciely

Lisa Danyluk

Nancy Lynn Dixon • Barbara Engelke

Bethany Fee • Vickie Gilman

Jennifer Juskiewicz

Anne Kirchhoff • Michelle Klos

Nicole Lauzon • Cindy Mahoney

Maggie McGee

Beverly Michaelsen • Pam Monast

Jennifer Shepard

2000-2001

Chairs

Ashley Jones

Beverly Michaelsen

Committee Members

Colleen Casto

Sabrina Mayfield

Susan McKee

Julie Ogden

Lindsey Patino

Jessica Pieters

Indee Rapp

Samantha Zeiders

Recipe Contributors and Testers

Debra Abbott
Liz Aladro
Laine Allen
Sylvia Allen
Carole Amos
Margaret Anderson
Anne Andreae
Bernadette Anile
Cathryn Ansbro
Kay Anselmo
Susan Armeli
Victoria Artel
Alison Ashmore
Linda Reid Askinas
Rachel Bailey
Jean Bass
Karen Bates
Amy Behrendt
Kathleen Bennett
Linda Bird
Debbie Bonefer
Barbara Bookman
Stephanie Boudin
Christine Boyer
Renee Branscomb
Jane Brobst
Paige Drummond Brody
Claire Brown
Ana Brushingham
Marci Buckles
Cynthia Buckley
Heidi Buitron
Cheramie Burgess
Debbie Burgess
Jane Burgess
Barbara Burke
Lauren Buschmann
Jean Cabot
Doreen Carlo
Patricia Carlson
Janet Carpenter
Heather Carroll
Tracy Carroll
Cindy Cast
Molly Cataldo
Christina Christian
Jana Cissel
Grayson Clark
Cindy Coningsby
Francie Connolly

Laura Cook
Mary Cooney
Ellen Cooper
Andrea Couch
Cyndi Coughlin
Susan Coyle
Loretta Coyne
Kathy Craft
Creative Cuisine Catering
Debbie Crum
Lou Daigle
Kathy Davis
Carol DeGraffenreidt
Veronica De Padro
Laura Depenbrock
Robyn Diaz
Nancy Dixon
Barbara Doll
Larissa Dorosy
Amy DuBois
Robin Dunn
Cynthia Shortle Economou
Natalie Epperson
Barbara Ericksen
Agi Fargas
Mary Lois Faulhaber
Nancy Fazio
Quinn Fazio
Bethany Fee
Nancy Fisher
Julie Flavell
Leslie Flavell
Liz Galatis
Miriam Gancitano
Sonali Garvin
Kimberly Geisland
Ann Ghattos
Allison Gilchrest
Victoria Gilman
Gina Goodrum
Susan Grant
Shannon Graulich
Angie Greene
Ann Griffin
Jane Grossman
Caroline Evans Guida
Katherine Guida
Kristi Haley
Sandra Hall
Sherry Hannaka

Elizabeth Harris
Laura Hatfield
Gretchen Heinsen-Acierno
Victoria Henszey
Ann Herrick
Dolores Hess
Lisa Hilowitz
Caryl Hippler
Suzanne Hollowell
Yvette Hooley
Jane Huston
Christine Immordino
Becky Irwin
Lynn Jenkins
Gennifer Jett
Sally Jezimir
Melodie Johnson
Linda Jones
Jane Katterhenry
Marion Kaufmann
Laura Kelly
Jennifer Kennedy
Tori Kennedy
Terry Kerr
Charlie King
Anne Kirchhoff
Gayle Kiser
Marty Kissel
Toni Kissel
Michelle Klos
Phyllis Korab
Roberta Kravitz
Wendi Kreps
Joanie Kretz
Clemmens Lachmayer
Graciella Lachmayer
Laura Lang
Rhita LaVine
Kim Liang
Carol Lieb
Joanne Liotta
Lori Livingway
Marcia Loecker
Begona Lozano
Eileen Macklen
Anne Madsen
Marianne Maffia
Barbara Mahoney
Cindy Mahoney
Suzanne Mandragona

Kristin Markham
Lucia Markowitz
Catherine Martin
Joan Martin
Debbie Mason
Sheryl Mauro
Alice McCarthy
Kathryn Camillucci-
McCollough
Catharine Meinson
Michele Meli
Kim Merk
Kelly Merritt
Julie Mersereau
Beverly Michaelsen
Daryl Middlebrooks
Victoria Mikels
Laura Minor
Janet Molehan
Leslie Monahan
Holly Moody
Joan Morris
Susan Murphy
Kim Nava
Genevive Niles
Mikey O'Neal
Alice S. Park
Lynn Drummond Parr
Ann Payne
Donna Pearl
Susan Pelike
Missy Pell
Maria Pierson
Theresa Puglisi
Robyn Rager
Jane Randanof
Susan Relicke
Cathy Richardson
Gwen Rinehart
M. Roche
Marie Rock
Kelly Rook
Susan Rotke
Pam Rower
Diane Rowlands
Nanette Rudolf
Betsy Russo
Jennifer Sacks
Andy Sarkisian
Heidi Schettler

Sandra Schoren-Testa
Cindy Schott
Mary Schu
Christie Schuh
Kim Schuh
Traci Schuh
Claudia Sciarretta
Sara Sears
Dee Selby
Nancy Sell
Janet Shanley
Heather Shaw
Kristin Shealy
Cathy Sheehan
Karen Sheldon
Kara Sher
Kendra Shortle
Jeannette Simons
Robin Slama
Colleen Smalley
Jane Smith
Liz Smith
Nina Smith
Susan Spragg
Sherrie Starcher
Dee Dee Stewart
Diana Stivor
Victoria Taylor
Nancy Theis
Sheri Thomasson
Deanna Thurlow
Jennifer Tkachyk
Ann Torino
Connie Vaughan
Maurice de Verteuil
Dee Dee Vincini
Mary Jo Walsh
Denise Weir
Christine Welch
Anne Welker
Beth Welker
Diane Wells
Paige Williams
Beth Winterholler
Debbie Wysocki
Joan Young
Sibba Zuelch
Susan Zykoski

Index

Made In The Shade

Junior League of Greater Fort Lauderdale, Inc.
704 Southeast First Street
Fort Lauderdale, Florida 33301
954.462.1350

Name

Street Address

City   State   Zip

Phone

Your Order	Quantity	Total
Made In The Shade at $22.95 per book		$
Sales tax at $1.38 per book		$
Shipping and handling at $4.00 per book		$
Total		$

Method of Payment: [   ] VISA   [   ] MasterCard
                      [   ] Check payable to Junior League of Greater Fort Lauderdale, Inc.

Account Number   Expiration Date

Cardholder Name

Signature

Photocopies accepted.